Just As We Were

Southwestern Writers Collection Series

The Southwestern Writers Collection Series originates from the Southwestern Writers Collection, an archive and literary center established at Southwest Texas State University to celebrate the region's writers and literary heritage.

Just As We Were:

A Narrow Slice of Texas Womanhood

Prudence Mackintosh

University of Texas Press, Austin

Printed in the United States of America
First edition, 1996

Articles that appeared originally in *Texas Monthly* are reprinted by permission.

Requests for permission to reproduce material from this work should be sent to Permissions, University of Texas Press, P.O. Box 7819, Austin, TX 78713-7819.

♾ The paper used in this publication meets the minimum requirements of American National Standard for Information Sciences—Permanence of Paper for Printed Library Materials, ANSI Z39.48-1984.

LIBRARY OF CONGRESS CATALOGING-IN-PUBLICATION DATA

Mackintosh, Prudence.
Just as we were : a narrow slice of Texas womanhood / Prudence Mackintosh. — lst ed.
p. cm. — (Southwestern Writers Collection series)
ISBN 0-292-75200-8 (cl : alk. paper)
1. Women—Texas—Social life and customs. 2. Upper class—Texas. 3. Texas—Social life and customs. I. Title. II. Series.
HQ1438.T4M33 1996
305.4'09764—dc20 96-11935

TO MY PARENTS, Ruth and J. Q. Mahaffey, who insisted that we validate life by writing letters home. Both the life and the writing were enhanced in the process.

Contents

Preface

I had lunch with a young journalist recently who confided that her education, her family background and expectations, her new friends, her old friends, and her own talents and interests were pulling her in five different directions. "Some days," she said, "I feel like a schizophrenic debutante." I could only suggest that she write about it.

The tensions she described have fueled my writing career and wrecked my closet for two decades. For all its frustrations, the opportunity to walk in many different worlds simultaneously is ultimately a gift. I first experienced it in the newspaper office where I grew up. Being the daughter of the town's newspaper editor gave me an insider/outsider mentality. I often knew the real story behind the headlines. My father's position also granted a measure of social prominence, but it never offered the financial underpinnings that such a position implies. My father's publisher paid our membership dues at the local country club, but I knew I couldn't order hamburgers by the pool. My debutante gown was my sister-in-law's wedding dress with the sleeves removed.

The University of Texas offered delicious anonymity to kids like me from small towns. It also offered the opportunity to add two or three more lives, with their own sets of friends. I had small-town friends I'd met at freshman orientation, with whom I was united by virtue of our Southern Baptist upbringing and our generally poor academic preparation. A favorite table in the Student Union Commons was for intellectual life with my English class cronies and professors. One professor christened me "Prudence, one of the Seven Deadly Virtues." Another life was entrenched in the Greek system—on Mondays we pledged ourselves in secret chapter meetings to pursue the ideals of "the beautiful and the good," and on Fridays we were matched with men (boys?) who escorted us to beer-sloshed basements where we writhed and howled to "Wooly Bully."

Rarely did these disparate lives intersect. If the Kappa pledge trainer had claimed to have seen me riding on the back of a bicycle with an unwashed, serape-clad beatnik en route to the truth-seeking Christian Faith and Life Community Center, I would have flatly denied it. Much to my embarrassment, one of my English professors confided that he once saw me crossing the campus wearing what he took to be a WAC uniform and was very shocked that I was pursuing a military career. Well, that was another life, as the sweetheart sponsor of an ROTC Military Police unit. In the hall between their bedrooms, my sons have a 1963 photo of me in full military regalia standing in front of an ROTC plaque that bears the inscription "Of and For the Troops." They are as puzzled as the English professor was about just what I did in the war.

Friends from all of these varied lives formed what I considered my intimate audience when I began writing for *Texas Monthly.* By the time I left Austin, I knew people from Borger in the Panhandle to Brownsville in the Rio Grande Valley, from Elysian Fields in East Texas to far west El Paso, an indispensable resource if one needs to know what "releathering a well" means or just how early baton twirling starts in Kilgore.

Many of the pieces in this book were originally unrelated magazine assignments. I went to the Hill Country to write about summer camps when I was twenty-nine. At thirty-two, I wrote about UT sororities. At thirty-four, I wrote about the Hockaday School, where I'd been a teacher upon first coming to Dallas. A couple of years later I wrote about my experiences in the Junior League, which prompted a lawyer from Beaumont to ask me if I had tackled a "Seven Ages of Women" series. He asked, "Will you follow the old darlings pottering about in their garden clubs as well?" I missed the garden club experience, but when *Texas Monthly* celebrated "the ties that bind" in its fifteenth anniversary issue, I did contribute a story about my book club.

In these early articles, I was writing about peculiar institutions that seemed to bind people together in the social fabric of Texas. What I see in rereading the pieces is that I was also writing the story of a young woman with rather strong democratic leanings who was sorting out the pleasures and perils of certain traditions that many of her contemporaries embraced without question.

All of these institutions have changed since I wrote about them, most notably the Junior League, which no longer has secret or exclusive admissions policies. Camps have retained rituals important to their alumni, but many have new owners and shorter sessions. Being assigned to the wrong tribe can still cause heartbreak in families. One woman, a former Tonkawa, told me that she'd requested her prayer group's intercession when she learned that her daughter had drawn "Kiowa" at Camp Mystic. Her sister and all of her aunts were Tonks. Hockaday once again has a strong headmistress. Sororities are still very much with us and seem as likely to disappear as does cheerleading in Texas.

The piece called "Help Wanted" is certainly not politically correct by today's standards, but the relationship between working women and their household employees continues to be intimate and awkward. In the late 1970's when I wrote this article, the term "nanny" was still exclusively British, and day care was Mother's Day Out on Wednesdays at the church. Readers responded with anecdotes that were more bizarre than those I recorded. Language barriers were often a factor. One woman returned from her errands to an acrid odor in the house. She found that the recently arrived Mexican maid was spray-starching the ironing with insect spray. Another San Antonio family reported that their sixteen-year-old son was the only one at home when their Spanish-speaking housekeeper went into labor. He drove her to the hospital emergency room, helped with the admissions procedure, and later discovered that his name appeared on the birth certificate as the baby's father. A Dallas family who displays their longtime housekeeper's studio portrait in the living room with family photos were hard-pressed to come up with worthy Christmas presents for her. One year, she requested piano lessons, which they arranged, allowing her to use their piano for practicing. The next year she said, "I love cleaning your house, but I'm too tired to clean my own." That year the family gave her her very own maid for Christmas.

"The Good Old Girls" had to be written on a very quick deadline, even though it would appear a full month after national weekly and daily publications had thoroughly covered the event. My chauvinistic premise was that the women's movement needed more Texans in charge. Liz Carpenter knew how to include everybody when she said, "I have known the warmth of a baby's laughter and, as a journalist, the satisfaction of a newspaper byline." Barbara Jordan with her biblical cadence touched the entire gathering.

Ann Richards' wit, charisma, and common sense made everyone listen up. Obviously, to my ear, these women's efforts at challenge and change had a pleasant Texas accent.

When I first started writing, my husband complained that I should be paid a "writer's depletion allowance" because I was gradually writing up every ounce of life experience I had. He didn't realize that the material never runs out here. I met a woman from far West Texas last year who introduced me to her new husband and added, "He's the greatest guy. He built me a little fence to keep the javelinas out of my pansies." Writers from duller states would kill for a line like that.

Prudence Mackintosh
November 6, 1995

Acknowledgments

Since many of these pieces were first published in *Texas Monthly*, I could not see them in print again without gratefully acknowledging that overworked original *Texas Monthly* staff who often responded to first drafts of these manuscripts with editorial suggestions almost as long as the piece I had submitted. Bill Broyles and Ann Barnstone were especially helpful to me as a young writer. So were the copyeditors and fact checkers with their diligent attention to detail and high standards for language usage. A friend once remarked, "I like the things you write, but never forget how much they are enhanced by their surroundings." Sassy graphics, clever headlines, and the incisive, thoughtful journalism that surrounded some of my stories brought me an audience of readers I might never have had.

I am also grateful to Joanna Hitchcock and Shannon Davies at the University of Texas Press for their abiding faith that there was a book worth publishing in all of this.

Just As We Were

The Soul of East Texas

MY EARS are attuned to the voices of East Texas, even though I've lived in the city for twenty years. "I oughta whup the tar outta you," I hear a mother tell her son as I finger the Jacksonville tomatoes at the Farmer's Market. I linger around the okra, hungrier for the expressions of my childhood than for the produce.

In a doctor's office, a man from East Texas tells me about his heart surgery. "Last year I was sick to where I couldn't hardly get out of bed." He is clearly enjoying the attention that his failing heart has attracted from important city doctors. "I was brought up hard," he explains.

The black woman shampooing my hair summarizes her sister's life and recent death in one confident sentence: "She did what the Lord gave her to do." I scribble the sentence in the margin of a magazine, tear off the scrap of paper, and put it in my purse.

Perhaps I am making up for the inattentiveness of childhood. With no other frame of reference, I, like most children, regarded the landscape of my childhood—East Texas—as ordinary. In 1956, my sixth-grade class celebrated the end of elementary school with a trip to Dallas, where we took in such extraordinary sights as Cinerama, the Health and Science Museum at Fair Park with its shocking plaster representations of a baby being born, and finally Love Field Airport, where I snapped a picture of Ed Sullivan rushing to his flight. That was the interesting world. Today, I would bypass the celebrity and take more notice of my classmates, some of whom may have had the tar whupped out of 'em, were being brought up hard, and might eventually do all that the Lord gave them to do.

I was born two blocks inside the Texas state line, in Texarkana. Like all Texas schoolchildren, I spent my seventh-grade school year studying Texas history and geography. I can sing "Texas, Our Texas," and I once performed a modern dance routine to "Deep in the Heart of Texas." Sitting on the public library steps waiting for my mother to pick me up, I gradually memorized one side of the inscription on Jim Bowie's statue: "Dreams of fabulous wealth lured Bowie to the San Saba region where he met with unexpected Indian attack." I was even a delegate to Bluebonnet Girls' State in 1961. My first writing effort appeared in the *Texas Junior Historian* magazine. Despite all those credentials, when I left the shadowy Piney Woods for the liquid blue skies and glaring limestone of Austin, I gradually realized that much of what I had grown up believing was Texan was actually Southern. The cherished myths of Texas had little to do with my part of the state. I knew dogwood, chinaberry, crape myrtle, and mimosa, but not bluebonnets or Indian paintbrush. Although the Four States Fair and Rodeo was held in my town, I never really learned to ride a horse. I never knew anyone who wore cowboy hats or boots as anything other than a costume. I knew farmers whose fences were bois d'arc and "bob wire" and whose property was known as Old Man So-and-so's place, not ranchers with their cattle brands arched over the entrance gates to their spreads. I knew ponds, not tanks. Streets in my town were called Wood, Pine, Olive, and Boulevard, not Guadalupe and Lavaca. Mexico was so remote that we called it Old Mexico. I knew people and a lot of things in only two colors—black and white. I quickly discovered that women who had grown up with less shade and more sky seemed less constrained than I was by the Southern dictum "What will people think?"

It did not occur to me until I read William Humphrey's 1964 novel, *The Ordways,* that my forebears in East Texas were perhaps the least adventurous of the Texas pioneers. Humphrey describes them this way: "Mountain men, woodsmen, swampers, hill farmers, they came out into the light, stood blinking at the flat and featureless immensity spread before them, where there were no logs to build cabins or churches, no rails for fences, none of the game whose ways they knew, and cowered back into the familiar shade of the forest, from there to farm the margins of the prairie like a timid bather testing the water with his toe."

Cowering back into the familiar shade? Timid bathers? Could I still boast of being a fifth-generation Texan if my great-great-grandfather Samuel Corley eschewed the vast and lonely Texas prairies to ride a Presbyterian circuit running just inside the state's eastern border from St. Augustine to the Red River? Since I grew up so close to the state line, in Texarkana, I've always feared that minor legislative gerrymandering might someday declare me an Arkansan. On the other hand, if the Corley family had charged on westward, their horses might have given out in Fort Stockton. I might have learned to sit a horse, but I would have missed the trees, the sandy-bottomed swimming holes, the hiding places, and the mystery indigenous to East Texas.

Historians have suggested that the trees in East Texas blocked our vision and walled us off from the outside world. From a child's perspective, trees were simply an integral part of our games. How could a kid in Fort Stockton play a serious game of Tarzan or Swiss Family Robinson or even hide-and-seek without thick trunks, vines, and pine needle carpeting? My mudpies were baked with mulberries or wild cherries. Chinaberries were ammunition. The partially exposed roots of an old oak tree could provide shelter for dolls or trolls or small plastic Indians. Magnolia trees offered totally enclosed play spaces, sturdy climbing limbs for even the smallest children, and cones with magic red-lacquered seeds.

Family and extended family provided additional shelter. Fourth and fifth cousins once or twice removed were counted as family. Family pride and the possibility of family shame were potent forces in East Texas. My father remembers being cautioned each time he left home, "Remember whose son you are." Who you were counted for more than what you had, and according to my grandmother, what you never wanted to be was "common." Texarkana was too big to harbor much of the clannishness or xenophobia that existed in smaller East Texas towns. A newcomer to these towns, even a much-needed doctor, might initially be welcomed with a flurry of Southern hospitality, but eventually the stranger would feel a chill while the locals withdrew to speculate on who his people were.

Families in East Texas were once bound not only by blood but also by certain traditions. My relatives could sing in four-part harmony, some could play musical instruments, and almost all could tell stories. Recently I had lunch with a handsome male cousin of mine who purports to be "ninety-two damn years old," and right there in Wyatt's Cafeteria, I got him to recite "The Ladies" from Kipling's *Barrack-Room Ballads.* Every time our family gathers, certain heartily embellished stories are told or at least alluded to. "The Rattling Fork," "The Dog on the Tilt-top Table," "The Day Mama Ran Away," "Uncle Burton and the Gideon Bibles," or the adventures of Troubador, a well-known dog-about-town who urinated on the preacher's leg during Chigger Corley's funeral, are all tales that cannot be written down. They are theatrical performances that demand raucous audience participation and may require the tale-teller to assume the countenance of a dog. My family's penchant for irreverent theatrical behavior was thought to be inherited and therefore unavoidable. Every time one of my brother's tales caused my Aunt Lois's legendary torrential cackle to erupt, he was rewarded by the family's acknowledging "Why, young J.Q.'s got a lot of his Uncle Burton in him." Certain strains in families are tenacious. Uncle Burton, who has been dead thirty-five years, was surely smiling somewhere the night my own small son, who could hardly lisp his own name, returned from the Rangers game imitating the bleachers vendors' "Co beah? Co beah?" I haven't decided yet which of my three boys will have to memorize Kipling's "Ladies."

Trees sheltered us and we were embraced by our families, but our churches taught us that all was lost if we weren't also "leaning on the Everlasting Arms." Although my roots were Presbyterian, and most of the family remained there, my particular branch strayed first to Methodism and finally to the First Baptist Church, the biggest church in town.

Ours was such an all-encompassing, full-service church that even in the days before Baptist bowling alleys and gymnasiums, we felt sorry for anyone who was not a Baptist. I regularly logged six or seven hours on Sunday and at least three on Wednesday night. No church made more demands on its young people or accomplished such measurable results. I was personally convinced of my wormy sinfulness and need for salvation at age seven. Anybody who attended church regularly and remained unbaptized by age nine was probably just not susceptible to Baptist pestering. The total-immersion baptism that followed a profession of faith before the entire congregation was performed in a giant fish tank set in the wall above the choir stalls. The candidates for baptism and the pastor wore white robes. The somewhat terrifying gravity of my own symbolic death to sin and resurrection to new life was lightened a little by my watching our preacher scramble into chest waders before performing the ceremony.

Once saved (always saved), we were lovingly goaded into memorizing vast amounts of the King James Bible. The Baptist Church taught us to listen, to speak and to pray before large audiences, to sing and to read music. We had to learn to dance and play cards on our own. Instead of slacking off in the summertime, the church doubled its efforts, with vacation Bible school and choir camps held at a Baptist encampment near Daingerfield. Church camp, with its prohibition against "mixed bathing," only heightened our awareness of sex and caused some to seek more passionate togetherness as "prayer partners" in bucolic thatched tabernacles appointed for private meditation.

Some who were brought up in the East Texas Baptist tradition remember only its hypocrisy and the burden of guilt that came from being dangled over the pits of hell on a weekly basis. My memories are more affectionate. The Baptists offered a child the security of a personal and loving God, a sense of democracy (Baptists vote on everything), a wealth of stories and hymns full of beauty as well as human frailty and gore ("There is a fountain filled with blood, drawn from Emmanuel's veins"), and the example of dedicated people who continued to care about you and probably pray for you even if you grew up to be an Episcopalian.

The evils of racial intolerance somehow never came up in Sunday school. I spent many a Sunday afternoon with the Baptist Girls' Auxiliary ministering to the children of gypsies, who lived in the worst poverty I've ever witnessed. The children smelled of urine and kerosene and lived in dark, tar-paper lean-tos on the edge of town. There were probably more stable, less dangerous neighborhoods of black families living in similar conditions, but we never went there.

Nevertheless, we naively prided ourselves on our close personal relationships with black people. I must have rocked a thousand miles next to Pinkie Satcher's ample bosom. Almost everyone we knew in our neighborhood of small houses had some help with the laundry and the children, which allowed lingering elements of Southern gentility. Maids polished silver, dusted cut glass, and starched tablecloths and napkins in exchange for unconscionable wages, bags of worn-out clothes, and bacon drippings.

We called them by their first names but also accepted their discipline. They seated us at the front of the bus and then matter-of-factly took their seats in the back.

We regarded them with an odd respect. Their hard lives gave them mysterious capabilities and folk wisdom that we didn't have. One of my older cousins credits his very existence to a black midwife who mixed a poultice of cobwebs and cow dung to stop the hemorrhaging from his umbilical cord. When I had babies of my own, I remembered their old wives' tales: "Don't hold your hands over your head. You'll strangle that unborn baby on his cord." "Bite that baby's fingernails off so he won't thieve." "Don't let him look in the mirror. It'll make him teethe hard." "Cross broomstraws in his hair to cure hiccups." We did not think much about their lives apart from ours.

To see East Texas clearly, I had to get away from it. For two summers of my college years, I worked in Washington, D.C., for Congressman Wright Patman, whose district covered eleven counties in Northeast Texas. I read and clipped news items from small-town newspapers and composed congratulatory letters to grim-faced couples in the district who were celebrating their fiftieth and sixtieth wedding anniversaries. Eventually I also read and helped to answer the stacks of mail that poured in daily. Those sad letters, written with knife-sharpened pencil stubs in quivery script on cheap tablet paper addressed to "Dear Honorble" or "Dear Congress" or " Dear Mr. Rite," revealed a poverty and illiteracy that I didn't want to believe. "Somebody sed you cud hep me. I don't see good and I can't hardly work." People in the First Congressional District wrote their Populist Democratic representative, who had grown up in the red dirt of Patman Switch, about their lost Social Security checks, their liver ailments, their no-account children, and their general despair that life could turn so bad. The last summer I worked there, 1967, I sometimes had to telephone grieving rural black women in towns like Tenaha or Bogota who had never been out of their counties and whose sons' bodies were now being shipped home from places in the world they couldn't imagine.

When I faced the level of need in my part of the state, the conservative politics that pervaded my high school civics class—the essay contests sponsored by the Daughters of the American Revolution on the threat of socialized medicine and the Communist plots seen in every welfare payment—seemed so blatantly hypocritical. Most of the people who petitioned Patman's office could *not* take care of themselves. Too often, local political powers in East Texas—narrow-minded county commissioners, sheriffs, wealthy attorneys, or judges—lacked the vision or inclination to do anything more than exploit or maintain the status quo. If the federal government did not help these down-and-out people, it seemed to me they had nowhere else to turn.

If going away from East Texas allowed me to see its people with wider eyes, it also afforded a fresh look at the natural beauty that I took for granted as a child. Driving toward Texarkana in the fall or traveling toward Marshall through Longview, I now appreciate the reds and yellows and oranges of the dense trees that line the highway. My husband's and sons' interest in fishing gives me time and places to admire bluebirds, hummingbirds, wildflowers, persimmon trees, snakey vines, odd mushrooms, and butterflies that flit in and out of dappled shade. But any foray into the lush countryside in East Texas is also likely to turn up equal parts of devastation—the sandy-bottomed creeks despoiled by salt water from oil fields or trash dumping, once-green slopes stripped for lignite coal and left rusty and eroded, dense hardwoods replaced with fast-growing, commercially profitable look-alike pines, and sweet-smelling air displaced by the acrid odors of paper mills. Quaint small-town squares are boarded up, their merchants unable to compete with the Kmarts and Wal-Marts on the interstates. Preservation and conservation are luxuries enjoyed by more prosperous, better-educated parts of the country. East Texas, struggling to keep its population employed, has never thought it could afford them.

I have to rely a lot on memory when I return to East Texas. Several years ago, while visiting my parents, I took my sons to see my first neighborhood school playground. A local kid doing handstands on the splintery seesaws challenged my boys. "Them ain't hard," he told them. "Y'all oughta try it." As if it somehow compensated for their reluctance to stand on their heads, one of my sons said to me in a stage whisper, "He speaks bad English." After their tour of my childhood haunts, which they found altogether unimpressive, they asked, "Mom, did you used to be a hick?" My urban children, growing up in an affluent, almost monolithic Dallas neighborhood, have temporarily presorted the world by economic status, blue jean label, educational attainment, and hairstyle into convenient categories—hicks, punks, airheads, and the rest of us. Without so much as a "Hidy, hy're you?" I fear that they indiscriminately lump my hometown folks right in with the worst crackers portrayed in *Mississippi Burning.* They lack the memory to see the people or the places as I do.

I cannot re-create for them the broader, intimate exposure to all sorts of plain and fancy people that small-town East Texas gave. I look at my son's school yearbook and compare it with my own. His class has a sameness about it—all clean, healthy-looking, college-bound kids with overpriced clothes, all knowing very little of the pain, poverty, and eccentricity in the world that I picked up just by osmosis. Leonard, who sat behind me in the second grade, had only one eye and sometimes delighted us by taking his glass one out at recess. Linda, across the aisle, sometimes had to see the school nurse about head sores. Some kids in our class were members of the Holy Roller church that didn't allow women to cut their hair. I daydreamed a lot about how long their hair would get before we graduated. Johnny's arm got broken when we were in the third grade, but his parents never had it set, so it always hung a little funny. Terry, who sat in front of me in the fourth grade, stepped on a rusty can, and since she had had no tetanus shot, she died of lockjaw. There was little fancy diagnostic testing then, and kids who now would be siphoned off into special education muddled right along with the rest of us. Through the years, tough kids with names like Bubba or Butch, with lopsided ears, missing permanent teeth, uncorrected crossed eyes, kids who would never shed "hisself" as a pronoun or "he done it" as an accusation, were as much a part of the taken-for-granted landscape of my childhood as the young Dillard's department store heir whose chauffeur drove us to country club birthday parties. If in my college years, I began to value philosophers more than plumbers, the balance was restored at my tenth high school reunion. I was eight months pregnant with my second child and could have been voted "Most Changed." A former high school football hero, whom I had tutored in English grammar, asked me to dance. Assessing my prominent belly; I lumbered out of my folding chair, smiled, and said, "David, you're awfully kind to ask, but you can't be serious." "Sure, I am," he replied. "I'm a butcher over at Safeway now, and I'm used to movin' big slabs of meat around."

My children giggle at the beauty shop sign "Chic Le Doll" as we turn down a street we always called Boulevard. I never had my hair done there, but seeing the sign recalls hours spent in small front-room shops that we called beauty parlors. Getting a permanent was an all-day affair, and in the course of the day an attentive child could hear enough bizarre gossip to frighten her out of ever growing up at all. I remember puzzling for weeks over the conversation about "twisted ovaries" and how Juanita "broke her water" right there on the kitchen floor before J.T. could get her to the hospital. Soap operas, another serious beauty shop topic, never quite measured up to the real-life sagas overheard while waiting for a final "wrench."

My boys see only the broken-out windows and the transients lounging in the lobby of the old Grim Hotel downtown, but I remember meeting former president Harry Truman there and hearing my father's glamorous stories of dancing to Ted Weems' orchestra in the roof garden, cooled by fans blowing over tubs of ice.

My children see a defunct boarded-up Union Station, with pigeons roosting near a clock that stopped maybe twenty years ago. But I hear whistles and deep-voiced stationmasters calling "All aboard" for Nash, Leary, New Boston, De Kalb, Clarksville, Paris. I remember the anxiety and pride of a summer excursion to Little Rock all by myself when I was only eight and an all-night train trip to Chicago by way of St. Louis with my best friend at sixteen for a summer at Northwestern University that inexorably changed our lives. Twenty-seven passenger trains a day once came through my town. My parents recall taxis honking and hotel agents from the McCartney and the Savoy Hotels vying for business out front. My father enriches the downtown picture for me with his memories of Sunday lunch after church at Huckins House, with its linen tablecloths and finger bowls. He remembers Al G. Fields' minstrel shows and Blackstone the Magician at the Ghio Opera House, where my sons and I now can see only a parking lot.

I visit aging neighbors for whom I am still a little girl, and my boys squirm with boredom. My children can't fathom how many people took a hand in my upbringing in a small town. There was no escape to anonymity.

East Texas has a mysterious hold on those of us who grew up there. In its flickering shade and light, it simultaneously revealed some truths and obscured others. We are left with paradoxes we cannot reconcile. How do I explain the love of language and a good story, the rural black speech rich with biblical "reaping and sowing and chastising," the relatives who once recited Tennyson, all coexisting with illiteracy and ambivalence about education? A music store in Dallas once ran a September special offering a shotgun with each piano purchase, an odd pairing of gentleness and violence that does not surprise an East Texan. In my childhood, the genteel little old lady across the street might be known for her wonderful heart and extravagant generosity, but she could turn from hugging me and say to her black maid, "I thought I told you I never wanted to see your black butt decorating this porch." Seeing a gracious mansion bulldozed to make way for a hamburger stand or a canopy of trees cut to widen a street near a dying downtown leaves us with questions about man's wisdom. Is it any wonder that I still hum *On Jordan's Stormy Banks* while I do the dishes and am simultaneously puzzled and relieved when a woman who has heard me give a speech says, "Honey, I can just tell you're anchored in the Lord."

The Greatest Experience of Your Life

"I KNEW I couldn't be a Pi Phi. I went to the wrong camp," the sophisticated Houston coed explained as we walked out of the Junior Ball Room of the University of Texas Student Union with respectable sorority bids in hand. The 1962 rush week "pig squealing" was over. For me, a small-town girl, it had been a week of unconscious blunders, naive assumptions, unwarranted overconfidence, and too much punch. I had been forewarned that I would need a jingly (preferably gold) charm bracelet to wear to the Pi Beta Phi rush parties in order to participate in the sisterly singing of "Ring Ching, Pi Beta Phi." The bracelet's symbols of high school accomplishments momentarily buoyed flagging small talk throughout the week, but there were status symbols that had not made their way to my rural province of East Texas. I had never been particularly concerned with Sakowitz and Neiman Marcus labels or Villager oxford cloth blouses. Pappagallo dress shoes held no majority in my closet. How was I to know about camp?

Certainly no one had asked me about the two weeks I had spent at Girl Scout Camp High Point in Mena, Arkansas, a healthy preadolescent experience that bore no resemblance to the camp stories I would hear about during my four years at the University of Texas. I gradually became aware that the camp one went to made a remarkable difference in all sorts of social endeavors, both in college and in the years that followed it.

My first visit to the Texas Hill Country around Kerrville convinced me that it is a camper's paradise. The cool, clear waters of the Guadalupe River are irresistible, and I waded in even before reaching the first camp on my tour. The hills themselves are part of camp life, since they provide a natural setting for secret "tribal" meetings. After you've heard the echoes bounce off Joy Bluff at Camp Stewart, you don't wonder that a Great Spirit could light the bonfire. With my feet in the Guadalupe, I lost a good bit of my skepticism about Hill Country camps. As one former camper put it, "All I know is, I thought about things on the banks of the Guadalupe that just wouldn't have occurred to me if I'd stayed in Dallas."

In a week I visited seven camps in the Kerrville-Hunt vicinity before going north to Inks Lake to see Camps Longhorn and Champion. I wanted to explore the mystique of the legendary girls' camps like Waldemar and Mystic. What was it about them that inspired such loyalty? Why would a college coed wear her diamond camp ring well into her junior year? Was it true that debutante bows were a part of the calisthenic program at Waldemar? Why did wives at lawyers' conventions or medical meetings greet each other with "Kiowa?" "No, Tonkawa"? Or why would a forty-year-old woman squint through binoculars across the Cotton Bowl and nudge her husband, saying, "See that blonde five rows up in the first deck? She was in War Canoe with me at Waldemar." What did these camps offer that would make a Texas daddy who had invested more than $12,000 in twenty-five cumulative years of summer camp for three daughters say, "It's a bargain"?

At fees of $465 to $650 per session (usually four to five weeks), all the private girls' camps along the Guadalupe offer a standard curriculum—swimming, canoeing, archery, riflery, horseback riding, tennis, crafts, tumbling, and dance. Some offer a great deal more. I couldn't help wondering if cheerleading appears as a regular activity in camps in Wisconsin or upstate New York—it does in Texas.

Girls' camps are emotional places. Take little girls away from boys for four weeks and they fall in love with each other. They adore secret clubs and tribes where they hug a lot and cry a lot and sing tearful, terrible corruptions of 1930's love songs or Broadway musicals. It's a confusing blend of Protestant Christianity and pantheism, with the word "love" used so liberally that a nine-year-old may not be sure whether she's crying because she loves Jesus, the Kickapoos, the tribal True Blue, or her counselor.

During my camp sojourn, I kept experiencing déjâ vu. I knew it couldn't be my old Girl Scout days, but it wasn't until I overheard a counselor saying, "We've got to get them to cry tonight, so they'll sign up for next year" that I knew. It wasn't camp; it was the sorority house during rush week, with the songs calculated to bring tears, the embraces, the rituals, and the ubiquitous Rodgers and Hammerstein scores.

One of my contemporaries, a Rice graduate, has always been puzzled and slightly amused by a University of Texas phenomenon. "Texas graduates," he says, "do not view their four years in Austin as a terminal experience." He theorizes that it is only a small part of a much larger picture, a place where paths begin to cross from all over the state in ways that will somehow affect the rest of their lives. I could hardly wait to tell him that though the bonding process is galvanized at UT, it does not always begin there. The words of the Houston coed came back: "I went to the wrong camp." I had unwittingly stumbled on one of the earlier threads in the continuum of Texas society.

A remarkably beautiful and healthy fifteen-year-old stands on the banks of the Guadalupe to give her inspirational vespers talk. She begins profoundly, "Two roads diverged in a yellow wood." Poor Frost. Would he enjoy the irony of his "The Road Not Taken" read on this hallowed camp ground? Camp, after all, is a decidedly decisionless place to be. As one ingenuous child said, "It's so easy to be good at camp." The other irony, of course, is that for most of these little girls the road is already chosen. It leads from Hill Country camp to private school, or at least to an affluent suburban high school, and then to what Texans regard as Eastern girls' schools: Mary Baldwin, Sweet Briar, Mount Vernon, Hollins, Randolph-Macon, or any of those institutions that offer the "Texas Plan." This plan allows girls to have one or perhaps two years out of state before returning to THE University, where they can live at Miss Hardin's (Hardin House, it's called now), acquire the necessary sorority credentials, marry lawyers, doctors, or inherited wealth, have two to four lovely, wholesome children, run car pools, dance a few years in the Junior League follies or work in the

Thrift Shop, and "knowing how road leads on to road," put their children on the appropriate waiting lists.

Counterparts of these Hill Country camps are dying out in the East. Spiraling expense, complaints from kids that camp is boring, and competition from shorter-term, specialized camps have taken their toll. Wilderness camps are so popular now that they can often charge more and offer less.

But the Hill Country camps don't seem to be suffering. To be sure, they have problems. Texas camps are currently fighting federal safety regulations, even though the ones I visited could probably pass the most stringent of inspections. I suspect the directors' real fear is that any federal interference not only will increase paperwork, and hence costs, but also might threaten their prerogative to decide who attends.

Kids themselves have changed in recent years, and this poses some challenges. Janis Joplin probably never envisioned "Oh, Lord, Won't You Buy Me a Mercedes Benz" as a song at Camp Kickapoo in Kerrville. Baseball teams at Camp Stewart have names like the Margaritas and the Harvey Wallbangers. Most directors agreed that their campers are more worldly wise and better trained athletically than in years past but certainly no more mature. Nurses said they are stocking as much Maalox as Mercurochrome, since many kids arrive with potential ulcers. They also said that more children are on prescribed medication than ever before.

No director would admit that drugs had ever been a problem at his camp, but all were extremely vigilant. A child at Heart o' the Hills was seen hiding a bag of white powder under her pillow, which a counselor quickly took to the director. Analysis at the Kerr County sheriff's office revealed that the bag contained ascorbic acid, a bittersweet candy substance. Si Ragsdale says that some of his campers wrote home with fictitious claims that they had discovered cannabis growing on Camp Stewart's property and implied that Mr. Ragsdale was raising a bumper crop. Kids are also more likely to challenge authority these days. "Why should I have to ride horses? I hate horses!"

Some camps are obviously bending with the times. Rio Vista for boys, established in 1921, seems to pay lip service to its Indian tribe traditions while actually becoming more and more a specialty sports camp. Its eight magnificent Laykold tennis courts reveal the principal interest of Jack McBride, Rio Vista's director and stockholder, who sees the possibilities of another tennis resort in the Hill Country. Increasing budgets and a dearth of "good help" are inescapable problems. The cost of sending a child to Camp Mystic increased from $575 last summer to $635 this year. Cafeteria food service has replaced family-style meals in all the camps except Waldemar, Kickapoo, Mystic, and Stewart.

In spite of problems and costs, these camps still have waiting lists. Most of the directors are talented salespeople, and their programs still please Texans. And camp has always been a safe place to park the kids while Mom and Dad are in Europe. But most of the parents I talked with suggested that they weren't so eager to get rid of the kids as they were to go to camp with them. A former Waldemar Ideal Girl whose daughter will soon be a camper recalled how safe and secure she felt at Waldemar. "I'll never forget the time some boys on motorcycles roared into our camp. I was near the kitchen and saw the cook run out brandishing his butcher knife after the hoodlums. I remember thinking, 'Gosh, they really *must* love us.'" These parents have terrific nostalgia for a place that is seemingly unchanged, for a time in their lives when life was uncomplicated by the responsibilities of adulthood.

Then there are the social implications. These camps are as close to boarding schools as most Texans will ever get, and they perform the similar function of introducing affluent children to one another. "Get to know the boys in your cabin, Son," one Camp Stewart father admonished. "Lamar Hunt was in my cabin and I didn't give a damn. Now I just wish he knew my name."

Heart o' the Hills, its roots in Texas legend, has fewer social pretensions than most of the other camps I visited. Built in the thirties as a lodge by Dr. E. J. Stewart, who was then the owner of Camp Stewart for boys and Camp Mystic for girls, Heart o' the Hills was intended to house the parents who came to Hunt for camp ceremonies. Arriving in the area without a hotel reservation, Dallas millionaire Colonel D. H. "Dry Hole" Byrd reportedly demanded a room at Heart o' the Hills. The clerk assured him that no rooms were available, so, in fine Texas fashion, Byrd turned to his companion, Kenneth Jones, a maintenance man from Camp Mystic, and said, "Kenneth, if I bought this place, would you run it for me? I need a place to stay." Jones agreed, and Byrd told the clerk, "We'll take it."

Jones and his wife turned the lodge into a camp in 1953. Its acreage is decidedly limited as Hill Country camps go, but the beautiful Guadalupe waterfront is accessible by tunnel under the highway, and steep hills rise behind the original lodge to provide the secret tribal ground for the Heart tribes—Pawnee and Shawnee. Although it has long been under different ownership, the camp's highest achievement award is still called Jo Jones Girl, a memorial to Jones' daughter, who was killed in a car accident.

Heart o' the Hills, now owned by Carl and Diane Hawkins, is the smallest camp I visited. It accepts 125 girls aged six through sixteen. The Hawkinses see the small size as a distinct advantage since it offers each camper a better chance to excel, as well as an opportunity to ride horses every day. Larger camps offer horseback riding only on alternate days.

The Hawkinses are hardworking people with extensive professional experience. Carl Hawkins loves what he does and has a genuine concern and sympathetic ear for every girl in the camp. The program is full, but relaxed, with particular emphasis on the kids' having a good time and making friends, rather than perfecting the final show for parents. The finale was in fact terrible—the craft display had the usual monstrosities: painted rocks, lapboards, and decoupaged plaques—but the little girls enjoyed it. Tribal competition between the Pawnees and the Shawnees is fierce throughout the session, but it is diminished somewhat by the joining of the tribes to form one Heart Tribe at the closing.

Additional hands to do the heavy or tedious camp work are scarce, expensive, and frequently unreliable, so there are few jobs that Carl and Diane Hawkins cannot handle, be it mowing grass, slinging hash in the cafeteria-style dining room, or counting up camp store deposits. Knowing who's who in Texas is simply not a part of the Hawkinses' experience, although their camp obviously draws from affluent families around the state and from northern Mexico. I returned from a neighboring camp one afternoon and mentioned to Hawkins that I'd seen one of Ross Perot's children. "Is that someone I should know?" he asked. Impossible? Not when you understand the news vacuum that exists in Hunt. Television and radio reception is so poor and the *Kerrville Mountain Sun* so completely local in coverage that it took me three days to learn that Fred Carrasco was dead in Huntsville. But it isn't just the inaccessibility of news that insulates you in Hunt. Camp is a cosmos unto itself. Nixon made his resignation speech on the closing day of one of the camp sessions while I was visiting. I was so involved in camp life by that time that I experienced some irritation that parents would delay the Memorial Vespers by refusing to leave their portable radios. Who cared about the American presidency? I wanted to know who had won the Jo Jones award.

"I learned a code at Waldemar that's almost a burden at times," the young woman told me. "Eight years at Waldemar taught me never to settle for anything less than the best in everything—pure quality—no veneer. I learned to do things thoroughly and to expect the same from others." She had been a camper at Waldemar sixteen years ago, and like an amazing number of women I talked with in Dallas, she felt Waldemar was one of the great moral influences in her life.

For sheer natural beauty, Waldemar's 1,200 acres along the North Fork of the Guadalupe in Hunt are unparalleled in the Hill Country. Architect Harvey P. Smith, who also restored the Spanish Governor's Palace and several missions in San Antonio, insisted that no trees be cut, and he designed native stone structures that seem to grow out of the hillside. Massive trees grow right through the roofs of several cabins. The masonry executed by German immigrant craftsman Ferdinand Rehberger in 1931 is matchless. The perfectly tended plantings suggest that the groundskeepers bear the burden of the Waldemar code, too. The Kampongs (cabins) are not carpeted or air-conditioned—which detractors had told me—but they have a certain spartan beauty: bunks are dark-stained oak, floors are red Mexican tile, and several cabins have fireplaces. The walls bear no names, carved initials, or tribal slogans. Since Kampongs are inspected twice a day, bedsheets had "hospital corners" and trunks were immaculate. The bathrooms, cleaned by maids, were sparkling.

August 1974 was not a good time to judge camp food. Rampant inflation could not have been foreseen when budgets were drawn up in the spring, but Waldemar was, typically, unperturbed by it all. None of the mysterious pizza, tamale, noodle, and Frito concoctions I had seen at other camps ever appeared in the polished dining room, where white-coated black waiters attended the table. The food is legendary: "I ate my first soufflé at Waldemar," a friend recalled. There are few packaged mixes, and the aesthetic manner in which the food is served is deemed as important as the nutrition.

But it is not only the setting and the food that set Waldemar apart from other Texas camps. Some say it's the Waldemar spirit, the immutable traditions, the social clout, and the intense loyalty it breeds; others believe it just may be Doris Johnson herself, owner and director of Waldemar and niece of its founder, Miss Ora Johnson. One friend admitted that as a nine-year-old she had believed that perhaps Miss Ora's ghost floated around the campsite at night.

"Waldemar is the only experience from my own childhood that I can offer unchanged to my daughter," one mother explained, as I needled her about having enrolled her newborn daughter for Waldemar in 1983. Tradition is a big drawing card for any Texas institution, and Texas traditions require only thirty or forty years to develop. The Hill Country camps, especially Waldemar, have made the most of it. The tribal rituals, the War Canoe picnic, and even a special Victorian vocabulary remain the same at Waldemar. Snack time is called "Nourishment," and who could forget Miss Roe, former calisthenics teacher, calling, "Boozerings up, whosits in, squeeze those legs together." Waldemar standards are traditionally rigid. Right and wrong are so clearly defined at camp that seemingly slight infractions may require a full confession before the entire tribe.

Waldemar offers the standard camp athletic activities, but with strong emphasis on perfecting form. Those who have attended camp long enough to participate in War Canoe, an exhausting activity requiring strength and impressive precision, can undoubtedly identify with the girl who said, "Every year after I got home from camp, I would turn my bare back to the mirror, lift my arms to a ballroom dancing position and watch with tears in my eyes as the muscles rippled across my back like Charles Atlas."

Even my most cynical friends became a little misty-eyed about Waldemar's tradition of traditions, the Ideal Girl Ceremony. The most loyal return year after year, well past their college days, to participate. The Ideal Girl is elected by the entire camp and staff at the end of a session, and her virtues are extolled in a candlelight ceremony that has not changed since the camp began. Once she is named, she is taken down the Guadalupe in a white canoe paddled only by former Ideal Girls while the entire camp sings, in choked voices, to "the spirit of Camp Waldemar."

Waldemar accepts girls aged nine to sixteen and has a capacity of 306. Present preenrollment applications will fill the camp through 1983. Grandmothers have been known to secretly enroll granddaughters whose mothers were still rebelling against their own upbringing. "Sally will thank me when little Sarah is nine years old." Although there is really no debutante bow practice at Waldemar, the social implications of going there are undeniable. Even the least enthusiastic campers admitted, "I wouldn't have thought of going through rush at Texas without my Waldemar ring." One former camper was amazed to hear a friend who had attended another camp admit that she had participated in skits satirizing Waldemar. "I was a little sad to think that they were so aware of us," the Waldemar graduate said. "We never even thought about them."

Indeed, Waldemar has experienced no competition from other camps along the Guadalupe, although "Nakanawa, in Tennessee, once took a lot of our Dallas girls," Doris Johnson conceded. Doris—she is known by her first name to all Waldemar campers—is the embodiment of the Waldemar spirit, high standards, and organization. Always clad in white, this slightly imperious doyenne of the Hill Country camps lives year-round in Rippling Waters, her home on the Waldemar grounds. She has been associated with the camp since 1928.

Doris maintained a certain aloofness throughout our conversations; as we strolled the grounds, however, it was apparent that she never forgets the name or face of any camper. When I mentioned my own contemporaries who had gone to Waldemar, she recalled not only their married names but also the names of their children. As I sat in her office looking at the massive wooden card catalog that records the pertinent information on every past camper, I couldn't help wondering how many of them regarded Waldemar as the last bastion of civilization. Perusing a Record Card, I noted that table manners are graded on a scale of 1 to 10. "Don't sixteen-year-old girls find this a little silly?" I naively asked. "It's more important than ever now; families eat on TV trays," Doris replied with ill-concealed disgust. I knew that Waldemar attracted girls from New Orleans and Little Rock, particularly during the second session, but I saw no evidence of the Mexican aristocracy from Monterrey, Piedras Negras, or Mexico City that I had frequently encountered at the other Hill Country camps. "We tried that once," Doris explained, "but we saw no need to continue. Their English was poor, and since most of them are raised by servants, they have terrible manners and are much too spoiled for camp life."

"What about notable or famous women who have attended Waldemar?" I asked. An icy hesitation suggested that I had trespassed. She replied with inoffensive though patronizing protectiveness, "No, I can't think of anyone who's made a name for herself."

What will become of Waldemar when Doris is gone? She is seventyish, and there is no clear line of succession. Wealthy parents and former campers, her loyal subjects, stand nervously in the wings awaiting her instruction.

If I asked a Mystic camper about the traditions she learned at camp, she would tell me about the tribes Kiowa and Tonkawa and the training rules—unchanged since 1928—that prohibit bare feet, Coca-Cola, candy, and talking at rest hours. She would tell about living in cabins called Chatter Box or Angels' Attic or Hangover, where her mother's name might be found carved in the rafters, or about tribal serenades or winning Best Posture.

"The Spirit of Camp Mystic is love," says Inez Harrison, the camp's director. "And that spirit pervades our whole camp. Mystic girls learn to love God first, others second, and themselves last." Before the day was over, however, I would know that Inez Harrison is no naive grandmother and that beneath the almost cloying sweetness there is a strong, intelligent organizer with a sound visceral sense of what these little girls need and what their parents expect.

Mystic has long been a favorite of the Texas political aristocracy. Texas governors Dan Moody, Price Daniel, and John Connally all sent daughters there. Lyndon Johnson's daughters were also Mystic campers. Luci unexpectedly took refuge here after the 1960 Democratic convention. Even now, Luci acknowledges Inez and Frank Harrison as her much beloved summertime parents.

Inez sees Mystic as a retreat. "The world demands too much sophistication of these little girls," she says. Outside that gate these same fourteen-year-olds might talk knowledgeably of birth control or the merits of the movie *The Last Picture Show,* but once inside, they are little girls screaming their hearts out for the Tonkawas. When they return to the real world, they might be a little embarrassed at this display of emotion, but for five weeks they can live without affectation.

Campers come from all over the state. Mystic also welcomes the children of Mexico's affluent families, but Inez admits that language and cultural barriers are not always so smoothly crossed. Imagine the trauma of a little Mexican girl being introduced for the first time to that relic of American pre-Freudian toilet training, the "Health and Happiness Chart," on which each child records her tooth brushing and daily bowel movements. One Mexican camper went for days without brushing her hair. The counselor hated to reprimand her, but by week's end, after swimming and riding horses, the child's hair was hopelessly matted. An older cousin was summoned to ask her why she hadn't brushed her hair. "I don't know how," the eight-year-old replied in Spanish. "My ladies have always done it for me."

Escorted by two counselors, I toured the camp grounds. Mystic's 650 acres on the South Fork of the Guadalupe are remarkably beautiful, but unmistakably camp. The cabins, although perched aesthetically on a hillside, are still no-nonsense frame or Central Texas stone with concrete floors. Indoor plumbing was added in 1939. A brief trail ride within the camp acreage took me through a clear creek and up to Natural Fountains, a curious basin-shaped stalagmite formation under a cliff, with natural springs bubbling up in it.

While observing the Mystic waterfront activities, I was startled to see a white Cadillac driven by what I took to be somebody's grandmother come barreling down to the water's edge. "Oh, that's just Ag," the counselors assured me. Agnes Stacey, an owner of Mystic and a camp personality since 1937, climbed out of her car and headed for the water. After a disciplined number of laps to and from the raft in the middle of the river, she climbed out, blue-rinsed hairdo intact. The counselors introduced me, and Ag said, "You know, I used to swim every day to the dam and back, but now they won't let me go alone, and these counselors can't keep up with me. You be at my house in about fifteen minutes. It doesn't take me as long to get into my girdle as you might think."

Born in Dallas in 1887 on a farm where the Cotton Bowl now stands, Agnes Stacey (then Doran) turned down a Dallas debut to attend the University of Texas, against her father's wishes. There she appeared on Cactus beauty pages, pledged Kappa Kappa Gamma, received a T Association letter in swimming, maintained a creditable academic record, and met Bill Stacey, a UT tennis champion. Her postgraduate days included graduate work at Wellesley, teaching school in France, and Junior League work in Austin. She and Bill took over Camp Mystic in 1937, possibly the worst time in American history to sell people on the importance of a private camp for girls.

It became apparent during my brief stay that Ag Stacey's stamina and her link with the Texas aristocracy are still a part of Mystic's continuing success story. The actual directing of the camp has been delegated to Inez and Frank Harrison, but this doughty octogenarian has not completely retired. She is still likely to appear in unexpected places doing unexpected things. Campers requesting a song from Ag after dinner may be astonished to see her climb up on the piano and belt out, "Oh, My Man, I Love Him So."

The camp calendar of activities is largely unchanged since Ag organized it years ago. Mystic offers twenty activities, of which campers select eight. The tribal competition in tennis, swimming, canoeing, and baseball produces amazing athletic prowess among the girls, but their energy is also channeled with equal zeal into cheerleading and twirling.

No one leaves Mystic without some sense of personal accomplishment. Even the klutziest kid can stand up straight for a week in order to win Best Posture or get fork to mouth efficiently enough to be named Best Manners. At Final Campfire, no less than thirty awards are bestowed, but there is no Miss Mystic. The honor that most little girls seem to seek is to return as a counselor. Former campers have told me that they were always aware of the counselor's sorority and that considerable preliminary rushing took place at camp. On learning my affiliation, Ag almost upset the mashed potatoes to slip me the Kappa grip across the lunch table.

Most of these private camps have recruiting parties at country clubs in the major cities. I attended a Coke party for Camp Arrowhead in February and couldn't help noting the disparity between the movies of sunny Arrowhead flickering on the screen before the well-groomed audience of mothers and daughters and the camp I had seen on a rainy day the previous summer.

Arrowhead is noticeably more rustic than Waldemar or Mystic and even a little bleak on a wet day, with muddy paths linking cabins that appear to have remained unimproved since the thirties. The heart of the camp is on very flat terrain, with only the clear Guadalupe and its cypress trees beautifying the site. When I saw separate bathhouses between the cabins, I thought to myself, "Now this is camp. These little girls don't mind roughing it." The cafeteria-style dining hall, called the Filling Station, suggested that eating was purely for nourishment. "Good manners are encouraged," one mother told me, "but Arrowhead doesn't try to be a finishing school. It's just a place to have fun." The only hint of social pretension that I saw at Arrowhead was the naming of the age divisions: Debs, Junior Debs, and Sub-Debs.

Arrowhead is by no means, however, an ugly stepsister of the other Hill Country camps. It offers similar, well-taught activities and equally adequate sports facilities, and it inspires great loyalty among wealthy alumnae across the state. Mothers who had gone to Arrowhead could hardly wait to start packing their daughters' trunks. "It hasn't changed a bit since I was there," one mother said. I could feel mothers around me thrill to Garner Bartell, camp director and owner, saying, "We're just as square as we've always been." Mrs. Bartell's family has been associated with the camp since its founding in 1934.

Arrowhead's tribes, the Kickapoos and the Pawnees, promote teamwork, leadership, and competition. A second-generation camper may choose to be in her mother's tribe, while others are assigned arbitrarily. Other than a few individual certificates and ribbons earned by campers, no awards are given at the Final Campfire. Mrs. Bartell feels that too many awards detract from the lifelong rewards of good camping experiences.

There are private boys' camps in the Hill Country, too. Stewart is widely acknowledged to be the male counterpart of Waldemar and Mystic. Silas B. Ragsdale Jr. exchanged his coat and tie for shorts and T-shirt when he left the Denton Chamber of Commerce in 1967 to become the owner and director of the socially prestigious camp, but he brought his super-salesmanship abilities with him. Touring Stewart's five hundred acres with Si in the camp's orange and white Ford Bronco, I learned a good bit about boys, Stewart's traditions, its problems, and its successes.

As we rode along, I could see that Stewart's site doesn't require much selling. The Guadalupe branches and bends to form four separate water areas—Blue Hole for fishermen; Bathtub, an area of shallow white-water rapids for nonswimmers; a Junior Pool with a Tarzan rope for average swimmers; and a Senior Pool for water skiing and canoeing. Joy Bluff rises above the Senior Pool and provides spooky echoes for nighttime bonfires. Younger campers' stone-and-frame cabins line the road that follows the athletic playing fields. Older campers stay across the river in Senior Camp.

Si's commentary made me well aware of the special problems that plague a boys' camp. He readily admitted that little boys are destructive, careless, and, most of the time, dirty. They will go to great lengths to avoid taking a shower and can mysteriously break four screens in their cabin during rest hour. "Now, that's what I'm talking about," he said, pointing to the broken window in the back of the camp station wagon. "That got busted during the dance with Waldemar, and no one is even sure how it happened."

Boys do not seem to form the emotional attachment to camp that little girls do, but that doesn't mean that camps like Stewart are devoid of tradition. Si stopped the Bronco long enough for me to meet "Mr. Lip," Stewart's favorite personality and link with the past. For thirty-five summers, Travis Lipscomb has served the camp in some capacity. Now, as head counselor, he remembers the good old days when "Uncle Bill" James directed Stewart. The place was much smaller then and campers much less sophisticated. "With Uncle Bill, the boys just did a lot of hiking and sleeping out," he recalls, "but now they require every day to be filled with planned activity."

Our next stop was the dining hall. Like Waldemar's, Stewart's bread is homemade and its cooks are a disappearing breed who use no packaged shortcuts. A little camper catching a small catfish in Blue Hole can usually persuade someone in the kitchen to fry it for him any time of the day. I saw the dining hall in action later that evening—a very different story from the kitchen. The noise even while the boys had their mouths full was earsplitting, and I saw one child stuff two pieces of bread into his mouth before trying to chew. Si apologized for the atrocious manners. "We make some attempts, but it's even hard to find counselors who know how to eat in public anymore." Former lieutenant governor Ben Barnes once won the Double Doily Award for having both elbows on the table while visiting his son Greg at mealtime.

Campers who attend Stewart for five years may get a second chance to polish their manners. Fred Pool, a former executive with the East Texas Chamber of Commerce and Si Ragsdale's longtime friend, takes a group of older Stewart boys for a week in Monterrey and Saltillo every summer during the camp session. Mr. Pool, who speaks fluent Spanish, introduces the boys to the cultural and culinary pleasures of Mexico, considered an essential part of a Texas gentleman's education.

The camp motto hangs on a wall in the dining hall: "Don't Wait Till You Are a Man to Be Great—Be a Great Boy." This is implemented with "Thoughts for the Day" and "Pow Wows," brief meetings at which distinguished visitors, counselors, or campers share their experiences. Stewart also offers its campers a chance to perfect their interests by bringing in specialists like "Rooster" Andrews to teach a football-kicking clinic, Rex Cobble for a calf-roping exhibition, or Steve Farish, professor of music at North Texas State University, for vocal instruction. The athletic clinics keep Stewart competitive with the sports specialty camps that have sprung up in recent years. But Stewart is interested in more than building athletes. As Si said, "Parents who send their boys to Stewart don't want their boys to be coaches, so we try to hire college students with professional ambitions, doctors or lawyers, to be in-cabin counselors."

Stewart accepts boys aged six through sixteen. The night I spent there, my maternal instincts got the best of me after I'd seen a stunt performance before a huge bonfire. The youngest campers, with meringue crusted in their hair from a pie-eating contest, looked too little to be away from their mothers for four or five weeks. But Kathy Ragsdale, the camp's business manager, handles homesick boys with aplomb. Giving an extra-warm hug to a little camper eyeing the Ragsdale telephone, Kathy, with her Sulphur Springs drawl, quietly comforted, "Sweetheart, we'll call your mama tomorrah. You just go on to sleep tonaht."

Tex and Pat Robertson, the executive directors of Camp Longhorn, are acknowledged by other directors to be Mr. and Mrs. Camp in Texas. Their operation in Burnet on Inks Lake offers three 24-day sessions each summer. Five hundred campers aged eight to sixteen fill each term. Everyone knows someone who's been to Longhorn, and that may in part account for its popularity.

In the truest sense of the word, Longhorn doesn't really qualify as a camp. As one young Stewart camper said, "My friends who go to Longhorn don't do very much that they couldn't do in Dallas." Longhorn campers don't go on overnights, seldom hike or even ride. (Longhorn has only thirty-eight horses.) Nature study is limited to a small petting zoo in the middle of the complex. Furthermore, it's hot in Burnet, with only an occasional scrub oak for shade. And yet, 1,500 kids can hardly wait to go back each summer. Tex says, "Longhorn is so many things—it's health, happiness, love of God and country, manners, friendship, and training in activity skills. It's also a place where young people can be counselors."

I talked with Tex briefly in his office before touring Longhorn. It had been a hard summer for him. Federal hearings in Washington on youth camp safety had been scheduled at a time when directors could least afford to leave their camps to testify. A contemporary of Gerald Ford's at the University of Michigan, Tex is suntanned, silver-haired, and physically fit.

Tex had so much to tell me about the evils of federal control that I hardly had time to get the basics on the camp. Longhorn for Boys and Longhorn for Girls are separate camps; however, Chow Hall is a common dining room, and occasional activities are coeducational. Former campers have assured me that they were very much aware of the opposite sex while at Longhorn.

Quite frankly, I have never seen so much teenage pulchritude under one roof as I did at Chow Hall. Features were regular, teeth straight, bodies perfectly proportioned. The most beautiful were the counselors, who were fairly easy to spot, since most wore sorority or fraternity T-shirts. Indeed, Longhorn seemed to be the most obvious prelude to UT Greek life that I had seen all summer; 64 of the 113 college-age counselors were from the

University. Orange and white colors everything from camp vehicles to sports equipment.

Longhorn is known principally for its water sports. Tex is a former Olympic swimmer, so it's not surprising that a timed mile swim is one of the major competitive events. Offerings include water skiing, water polo, diving, scuba diving, and "blobbing," a Longhorn original. Created by boys' camp director Bill Johnson, the "blob" is a huge orange and white, whalelike inflated plastic float. It is much like a trampoline, though much harder to stay on.

Another popular activity at Longhorn seems to be collecting Merits, small plastic tokens earned by good behavior, that are negotiable only at the camp store. The store is a child's fantasy world of sporting equipment—not just baseballs and Ping-Pong paddles but ten-speed bicycles, water skis, and expensive tennis racquets. A kid seldom stops to realize that merits sufficient to purchase a bicycle would probably require attending camp at least eight years, which would cost his parents approximately $4,000. Merits are also sent to Longhorn campers on their birthdays. Around Christmastime, a staff member delivers the *Longhorn Yearbook*, a thick orange-and-white volume containing pictures of the campers and counselors and candid shots of the past summer. During this visit, the staff member inspects the camper's room; for every memento of Longhorn found there, another Merit is awarded. Recruiting carnivals at country clubs in major cities allow prospective campers to win Merits playing games. This merit system is apparently so successful in keeping misbehavior down and camp attendance up that it has been adopted by neighboring camps like Champion, a newer camp that boasts Darrell Royal as a stockholder.

Longhorn's site is almost as crowded with buildings as the University of Texas campus. Enough cabins to house five hundred somehow diminish the feeling of wide-open spaces normally associated with camp. Longhorn's only claim to real rusticity is that cabins lack electricity and running water. (But bathhouses with both are less than ten yards away.) Well-tended carpet grass makes shoes superfluous.

Aside from the chance it offers to glimpse the opposite sex, the dining hall is a purely functional cafeteria. Campers eat on metal army-type trays, which they must wash after each meal. A Waldemar camper who later served as a counselor at Longhorn said, "My father almost didn't let me stay after he saw the food. I couldn't write him that part of my duties as counselor included clipping the hedge."

Counselors told me that they felt a strong obligation to keep the kids happy and entertained. Longhorn is not big on tearful sentiment, and its closing ceremonies are quick and painless.

[So is this ending. . . . This article was half essay/half service piece for a very young *Texas Monthly.* At the time I wrote it (1975), I did not envision subsequent articles on sororities and the Junior League.—P.M.]

Why Hockaday Girls Are Different

IN MY SMALL East Texas town in the late fifties, admitting that you went to Hockaday was just a cut above confessing that you had done time at the State School for Girls in Gainesville. From my provincial fifteen-year-old perspective in those tranquil days before court-ordered integration and busing, the only plausible reason for sending a girl away to boarding school was her delinquent behavior. Some boys from wealthy families in our town went East to Exeter or Andover for academic or social reasons, and other males with less promise got "straightened out" at Allen Academy, Peacock, or the Texas Military Institute, but the unruliest girl I ever knew was dispatched to Hockaday. And when she came home at Christmas and crashed a party at the country club, chain-smoked, drank Scotch on the rocks, and performed a totally uninhibited dirty bop in front of the chaperones, we thought she was a wondrously sophisticated creature.

Imagine my surprise in the early sixties to find Hockadaisies in my sorority pledge class at the University of Texas. Making my way at the big university as a small-town kid, I naively assumed that I would have a lot in common with small-town girls from equally distant provinces in West Texas or the Panhandle. I was wrong. My sisters from Wichita Falls were chicly coordinated by Neiman Marcus, and to my amazement a girl from Amarillo had recently been photographed by the French fashion magazine *Réalités.* The photograph that identified me during rush was straight from the "Best All-Round Girl" section of our Texarkana Tiger yearbook; their pictures with the wistful expressions, garden party hats, baskets of flowers, and white organdy dresses looked to me as if they had been painted by Renoir. I later learned it was Gittings, the photography studio at Neiman Marcus. And besides daddies who dabbled in cattle or oil or just money, the main thing we did *not* have in common was the Hockaday experience.

As I got to know these young women, I quickly perceived that not everyone who had boarded at Hockaday was a behavior problem. Indeed, a Hockaday teacher would later say of my 1950's acquaintance, "Leg irons could not have restrained that child." In all honesty, however, it did seem to me that these girls from Hockaday were decidedly less awed by the restrictions set by the university or sorority than I was. I would later realize that a great deal of energy in boarding school is spent trying to get around school rules. So while I doggedly attended every class—even at eight o'clock on Saturday morning—and worried about getting caught if I attended a party in an off-campus apartment or about being locked out of the sorority house after hours, they blithely slept late, played a lot of bridge, obtained unauthorized snacks from the kitchen, or called the Chicken Delight delivery boy, who agreed to attach boxes of chicken to a string of brassieres lowered from the second-story window. If they did attend an early-morning class, it might be in trench coat thrown over nightgown, a tactic learned at Hollins or Connecticut College on the "Texas Plan." And if the sorority house door was locked when they chose to exit or enter, it was a simple matter to use the downstairs bathroom window. While we drones carefully memorized the sorority rituals, they created hilarious, irreverent parodies of the sacred ceremonies and held mock initiation rites that included their screeching like owls in the presence of bewildered, blindfolded pledges. They sometimes disappeared for weeks at a time to participate in the Tyler Rose Festival or to make their debuts, and when the days of reckoning, exam week, came, these spirited grasshoppers seldom had to pay. Their rigorous high school preparation—or was it their inherent glibness?—enabled them to write English and history papers with minimal effort. Or if worse came to worst, they knew where to get Dexedrine for an all-nighter before the exam. You didn't have to go to Hockaday to know these things, but I think it helped.

In 1969 I had my chance to go to Hockaday as a teacher of eighth- and ninth-grade English. Although by that time I had acquired a measure of sophistication by working in Washington, spending a summer abroad, marrying an English major turned lawyer, and teaching for four years in an Austin public school, I was still mightily impressed with the trappings of this legendary private school. My earliest letters to my parents after I assumed my teaching job recall a headmaster's dinner with standing rib roast, Caesar salad, and crème de menthe pie. A buffet dinner with resident students and their parents whose name tags read like a Texas Who's Who was no less sumptuous—chicken Kiev, ham rollups, green rice, plus silver trays of cold shrimp and fresh fruit. Dessert was a fluffy lemon mousse with toasted almonds. Clearly I was done with the gristly Sloppy Joe burgers and Jell-O of my public school teaching days. Gone, too, were the smells of every school building I had ever known. In the cool, glassy elegance of this shiny modern structure, there were no sweaty, scruffy children with unwashed heads, no odors of bologna or overripe bananas in sack lunches; the chalk dust disappeared from my chalk tray daily and I never dispatched students to clean the erasers.

Of my students, I wrote home,

> *They seem younger than my public school students, perhaps because single sex education does free little girls to be little girls longer. Seventh graders still bring their jacks and jump ropes to school and the playground monkey bars are full of eighth graders during our morning break. Their enthusiasm for their Green and White athletic competition is phenomenal. They even elect cheerleaders for their teams. I suppose somehow I always associated cheerleading with the male-female mating ritual in public schools. I also had assumed that girls were sent to Hockaday to avoid that kind of inane activity. My eighth-grade girls are as giggly as I expected, but polite and manageable. Students at Hockaday stand when the headmaster or a faculty member enters the room. I still can't get used to referring to the ninth graders as First Form. This preppie labeling of the Upper School grades strikes me as a bit pretentious in Texas. In response to my suggestion that they inform me of any special problem they had that might hinder their success in the class, I received this note:*

> *"Mrs. Mackintosh, Please don't let me bite my fingernails in class. I know you wouldn't like to look at me chewing my fingers so please help me to stop this awful habit." Since my duties also include policing their manners at the lunch table, I will feel more like a governess than a teacher by the end of the year.*

Occasional references during that year to "my horses," or "when we got back from Christmas in Guatemala," or "the summer we rented the cottage in Provence" reminded me that, for the first time in my brief teaching career, I was no longer a role model. I often worried about the world history teacher who taught them about countries that they knew firsthand but that she had only read about. I sometimes left at the end of the day wondering what business I, with a B.A. from the University of Texas, had teaching thirteen-year-olds whose life plans already presumed acceptance at Smith, Vassar, Wellesley, or Radcliffe—schools I had never heard of at their age. How different our educational experiences were. They would never know the frustrations of being taught world history by a football coach, nor would any of their classmates become grocery store checkers or beauticians after graduation. I once put aside the *Odyssey* to read my students a poignant Larry King short story from *Harper's* about a carhop. Perhaps I reasoned that with little assistance from me, Hockaday girls might meet noble Greeks on ships, but never would they encounter a carhop with a boyfriend in Vietnam.

Miss Ela Hockaday, the school's founder, had died thirteen years before I came to Hockaday. Indeed, she had taken no active part in the administration of the school since retiring in 1947. But her influence was still apparent even to those of us who were too busy, or too young, to be interested. A tall, fragile lady named Miss Bess Funk, whose primary function seemed to be greeting guests in the foyer and carrying the mail from office to office in a wicker May basket, was one obvious link with the past, as was Miss Kribs, a 1921 graduate and former Idlewild (the premier men's social club of Dallas) debutante who had been in continuous employ of the school for forty-eight years. I was warned about her the day I arrived. Everyone said the same thing. "Miss Kribs is worth her weight in gold. She saves the school so much money by accounting for every paper clip, but you might save yourself some sermons and tongue-lashings by purchasing your own supplies." Miss Kribs wore her hair in a net and reminded me of a bulldog. Her seniority gave her certain liberties. I noticed at once that she called all of the teachers by their last names, drill-inspector fashion. More than once I saw the headmaster, Robert Lyle, stop dead in his tracks when she barked, "Lyle!" I checked my book orders for Miss Kribs more carefully than I did my students' papers. Pity my colleague who went to the book-room to fetch her classes' copies of Lorraine Hansberry's *Raisin in the Sun* only to find that Miss Kribs had ripped the front covers off. "Joyce [her last name], you didn't tell me you were ordering books with coloreds embracing on the front. I cleaned them up as best I could," growled Miss Kribs.

The most obvious legacies from the past at Hockaday are the Memorial Rooms—the Great Hall, the Memorial Dining Room, and a small library room—antique-furnished shrines from the old Greenville Avenue campus now encased in the suburban ultramodern Welch Road structure. The rooms were not used much by students when I was there. Teas were held in the Great Hall and the student council was allowed lunch in the dining room once a week, but the rooms had an off-limits, museum quality that discouraged curling up in a wing chair to finish reading *Anna Karenina.* And to me, who at twenty-five was not untouched by the iconoclasm of the sixties and who knew so little of Hockaday's tradition, they seemed an enormous waste of money and space.

Eight years later, I now know that there are several things about Hockaday that you can't understand if you are still, despite being warned, washing your grandmother's hollow-handle silver knives in the dishwasher; or letting the baby take Great Uncle Harry's silver rattle to Six Flags; or yawning when your mother-in-law tries to explain her latest find in the genealogy charts. Part of Hockaday's story presupposes that you know the importance of beautiful things and care about continuity from one generation to the next.

To learn about Hockaday from those who have known it the longest, you have to go to what is, by Texas standards, "the old money." Their homes have warm, gracious living rooms or libraries where, despite your intention to be an objective journalist, you cannot resist becoming a relaxed guest. Tea is served in cups that, like grandmother's knives, must be handwashed, and the cookies are crisp homemade almond tuiles. There is an assumption that everything should be as lovely as possible—not ostentatious or extravagant, but simply harmonious and elegant. And in the homes of these early alumnae and benefactors, it is.

In the memories of some of these alumnae, and even in the Hockaday history, a somewhat flowery tome published in 1938 to commemorate the school's twenty-fifth anniversary, Miss Ela Hockaday looms larger than life. "To this day," one alum of the twenties recalled, "I still remember Miss Hockaday chiding me about being on time. Once when I came downstairs late for dinner once again, Miss Hockaday actually cried. I'm very punctual these days." Over and over again, I heard women say, "She was my mother's very best friend" or "She was such a lady." That she was the consummate lady, I have no doubt. That she was anyone's closest chum is debatable.

Ela Hockaday was a native Texan, daughter of a rigid, scholarly schoolmaster who had an academy in the small East Texas town of Ladonia. Her mother died when she was a child, and her older sister aided their stern father in caring for her. Except for a brief stint at Columbia University, she obtained her formal education in Texas teachers colleges. She gained some prominence as a teacher by taming ruffians in the Sherman schools and went on to teach at Durant Normal School before coming to Dallas. I assume that her unerring taste and sense of decorum were inherent. On the recommendation of M. B. Terrill, whose Terrill School for boys was a forerunner of St. Mark's School of Texas, now one of Dallas' most prestigious private schools, Miss Hockaday was summoned in 1913 by Dallas citizens H. H. Adams, Ruth Bower Lindsley, and "others" to establish a college preparatory school for girls.

Noted for her quick, incisive mind, Miss Hockaday must also have been a capable politician. "The perfect casting for the Virgin Queen" is the way Stanley Marcus remembers her. In no time at all, she had assembled a privy council of Dallas' most powerful civic leaders that included names like Charles Huff, R. W. Higginbotham, Charles Kribs, and Herbert Marcus. (Later Hockaday boards would include theater magnate Karl Hoblitzelle, oilman Jake Hamon, and the founders of Texas Instruments, Eugene McDermott and Erik Jonsson.) Stories abound about these men leaving conference rooms to do Miss Hockaday's bidding. Some of them provided legal advice, others had financial connections and business sense to offer. Most of them also had daughters. Herbert Marcus Sr. had only sons, but it is easy to see why Miss Hockaday sought his counsel. At a testimonial for him in 1937, she said, "Mr. Marcus has carried artistic value into whatever he has done." In a sense, Miss Hockaday and Neiman Marcus were in similar businesses. In that same testimonial speech, she went on to say, "The women of Dallas have always felt grateful to Mr. Marcus for giving them utter confidence that their clothing was appropriate and tasteful wherever they were, whether in Dallas or in a city that was a world capital." Miss Hockaday's job was to see that the confidence Dallas women had about their appearances would not be undermined when they opened their mouths.

With meager financial backing, Ela Hockaday opened her school to ten students on September 25, 1913, four days after she arrived in Dallas.

In those few days she had located a house on Haskell Avenue for the school, hired her teaching colleague and friend Sarah Trent as faculty, and devised a curriculum that included mathematics, English, history, Latin, German, and French. Twenty-eight years later, the *Christian Science Monitor* noted:

> *Miss Ela Hockaday has accomplished the so-called impossible. She has made a private school pay its own way, unendowed and not tax supported. . . . Today [1941] she is president and active head of a school with a student body that numbers 450, a staff of 83 and a plant approaching a million dollars in value, still unendowed, still the complete servant of its president.*

The lack of endowment and Miss Hockaday's iron-clad reign over the first thirty years of the school's life, so lauded by the press, would plague her successors. To this day, headmasters at Hockaday are regarded by some who were intimately acquainted with the school in its early years as unworthy pretenders to the throne.

Hockaday quickly outgrew the small house on Haskell near downtown and moved to a nine-acre portion of the Caruth farm on Greenville Avenue and Belmont, which then was the outskirts of Dallas. From alumnae scrapbooks, I can piece together a pleasant picture of Georgian buildings, Miss Hockaday's antique-filled cottage, rose gardens, a swimming pool, playing fields manicured but frequently scarred by hockey sticks, and "the pergola." (I confess, I had to look it up too.) In a description of the grounds at Hockaday for the 1938 history, Isabel Cranfill Campbell ('27) writes,

> *Way back in the beginnings of Hockaday there was the pergola . . . an inspiring place always, with its sweeping view of the campus which has twice received a civic prize for beauty. Here the yearly round means an exchange of blossoms—forsythia and redbud at winter's end, jonquils in the new spring grass, valiant zinnia borders at mid-*

summer, and autumnal chrysanthemums. Only the clematis vine that wreathes the pergola itself is renegade. For, constant as the Northern Star, it refuses to bloom until just after Commencement, when school is out and it must waste its sweetness on comparatively desert air. Still and all, such happy progress has been wrought here, the school has grown so lustily and well in all its parts, that I, for one, expect one day to see the clematis change its stubborn mind and send out white fragile blossoms to honor the graduates of Hockaday.

With such florid prose in my head, it was depressing to walk around the undistinguished Belmont Towers apartments on Greenville, which rise now where Hockaday stood until 1961. Only a hedge from the old school remains. However, some of the merchants in the area haven't forgotten Miss Hockaday. Bill Clark, of Clark's Fine Foods, the market that provided Hockaday's food on the old campus, still recalls Miss Hockaday's inviting him to her cottage to meet Eleanor Roosevelt. With a sheepish grin, he also recalls, "I had a bad habit. Well, I guess I still do. When I'm making change, I lick my thumb to separate and count the dollar bills. I can still hear Miss Hockaday saying, 'Bill, don't do that. You never know who's had their hands on that money.' "

If Miss Hockaday felt she could inflict her standards on her grocer, you can imagine the scrutiny she gave her students. Her school was begun in an age when, at least in Texas, there was no ambivalence about moral imperatives. To understand Hockaday's early days, you have to assume the nineteenth-century mentality of its founder. All things were achievable with self-discipline and hard work. M. B. Terrill of the Terrill School was widely admired in those frontier days as a headmaster who brought student transgressors to swift and terrifying justice. Although Miss Hockaday did not pounce on her girls and belabor them with blows as Terrill did his boys, she was a stern disciplinarian nonetheless. One longtime associate of Hockaday admitted that there were times when she wanted to stick her tongue out at the stiff headmistress. "She was absolutely uncompromising in her standards and you either embraced her code or you had nothing to do with her school."

So that she might detect any student infraction of the "no smoking" rules on the Hockaday campus, even the gardeners had to comply. Maids who cleaned the resident students' rooms and served the seated meals were to be impeccably uniformed. "After cleaning up Trent House, we were supposed to get ourselves cleaned up, put on our formal serving uniforms, and be sure our shoes were shined. Everybody 'dressed' for dinner at Hockaday," Exie Tunson, who worked as a maid for Miss Hockaday for thirty years, proudly recalls. Not only did Miss Hockaday prescribe the schoolgirls' uniform—middy blouse, bloomers, black stockings, and high-top brown-leather "cow shoes"—but she passed judgment on the girls' street dresses and ball gowns. Delivery trucks from Neiman Marcus sometimes brought the long boxes containing prom dresses first to Miss Hockaday's cottage. At the tea dances, if she detected alcohol on the breath of any young man, he was blacklisted from further participation in Hockaday social functions. Indeed, some of the earliest graduates recalled that no men were allowed at dances at all. The girls danced with each other and, to this day, some admit, they have to consciously remember not to "lead."

Hardly anyone remembers being scolded by Miss Hockaday; it simply wasn't necessary. Her awesome presence was usually enough to correct any irregular activity. Exie Tunson remembers serving coffee to the faculty after dinner in one of the rooms not far from the study hall. "We'd close the doors and all have a ball in there," Exie recalls. "One night, Miss Winifred Clopton was playing the piano, and I said, 'Miss Wini, play the St. Louis Blues.' And boy, she wailed away on the St. Louis Blues. And Miss Gulledge and Miss Dolly and a bunch of us, we were all trying to sing low all about 'got the St. Louis Blues' and Miss Hockaday opened the door. Oh, boy! It was like a bunch of roaches when you turn on the light."

A similar story comes from an early boarding student. She and her roommates dared to sneak back into the kitchen after lights-out for an additional serving of ice cream. Just as their spoons were digging into the large ice cream can, the lights went on. There stood Miss Hockaday in her bathrobe with flashlight in hand. "Oh, girls," she said sweetly, "You must still be hungry. Well, this is certainly no way to eat. Put those spoons down." With that, she summoned a maid and instructed her to put on a uniform and to set the table with linen place mats, napkins, crystal bowls, and spoons. The errant boarders were led to the dining room and required to choke down two bowls of ice cream before returning to their rooms. No scolding. Just a presence powerful enough to scotch any signs of rebellion within her realm.

Those were the days when rebellious girls seamed-in their middy blouses with safety pins or waved at the Terrill School boys who circled the campus and sometimes left notes in the columns out front. Surprisingly enough, some of those with the safety pins in the seams of their middies have the warmest recollections of their days at Hockaday. "She gave me hell," says one who is still something of a rebel, "but I admired her because she was tougher than I was, and she never held grudges. She came to my wedding even though I married a man she had blacklisted for responding improperly to a tea dance invitation. Actually his roommate at SMU had responded to the invitation for him—on toilet paper."

Miss Hockaday attended a lot of weddings. And even the husbands of Hockaday graduates can often tell you what Miss Hockaday sent as a wedding gift. The wives can also tell you how it was wrapped and whether she brought it personally or had Sam, her chauffeur, deliver it. Her gifts invariably became family treasures. An inveterate collector, she almost always gave pieces of antique silver, sometimes from her own collections. "Thanks to Miss Hockaday," one early graduate says, "many of us who graduated in the twenties are 'silver and china rich.' The Depression was already hitting Europe, and many fine European families were having to liquidate their assets. Miss Hockaday encouraged us to invest in these treasures." Always a frugal woman, Miss Hockaday supported herself during lean years with her antique collections. "If she needed a little money," Exie Tunson says, "she'd just sell off a little Rockingham china."

If Miss Hockaday seems a little stuffy, it may be because I had such difficulty getting what I felt to be a complete picture of her. Even those graduates who returned as married adults to have dinner at her cottage admit that they never quite felt relaxed enough in Miss Hockaday's presence to partake of the preprandial martinis and cigarettes she proffered. If she had any sense of humor, no one I talked with could specifically recall it. They remembered her intelligence, her probity, her self-discipline, her kindness, her concern for each of her students, her impeccable taste, but no one seems to remember a time when she took herself less than seriously or displayed any vulnerability. Helen B. Callaway, of the *Dallas Morning News*, recorded a favorite vignette about Miss Hockaday in a fiftieth anniversary story in 1963:

> *On the third day of World War II, the news wire had chattered out a sizzling story that was to send American blood pressures soaring: A German submarine had torpedoed and sunk the British liner SS* Athenia, *with 1,418 people aboard, including many from the United States. A number were Hockaday students.*

Reporter Fred Zepp called Miss Hockaday late that night, rousing her from sleep to break the news of the stunning tragedy at sea.

After the briefest of pauses, Miss Hockaday commented: "That seems highly irregular."

Perhaps the maintenance of very high standards always requires a little stuffiness. And sometimes Miss Hockaday's highly valued code of self-discipline went to extremes. The story is told of a Latin teacher, a spinster, as most teachers were in those days, who came to Hockaday from Virginia. She brought with her the exquisite antiques accumulated by generations of her aristocratic forebears. She was just the sort of refined woman Miss Hockaday valued as a model for her girls. "Self-control is the mark of a gentlewoman," preached Miss S. And she demonstrated it most dramatically one day when a breathless student interrupted her class to announce that Miss S's apartment was on fire. "Is the fire department there?" Miss S calmly asked. "Yes," replied the excited student. "Very well, class, we will continue our declensions." The teacher lost everything in the fire and was generously taken in by a day student's family for the remainder of the term. That she hanged herself after graduation that year is a sad commentary on the virtues of gentlewomen.

The parents who brought Miss Hockaday to Dallas wanted a college preparatory school for their daughters, and she obliged by sending members of her first graduating classes to such schools as Barnard, Smith, Radcliffe, Wellesley, Mount Holyoke, Stanford, and Vassar. As there was no ambivalence about proper conduct for a young lady, Miss Hockaday had no lack of conviction about what belonged in a woman's education. She based her school on what she called the Four Cornerstones—Scholarship, Courtesy, Athletics, and Character. According to a 1928 graduate, "Hockaday gave me the nuts and bolts for building a very satisfying liberal arts education. In those days we were never asked to do anything particularly creative. There was too much to be learned and I guess we were vessels to be filled. I know that's not a popular educational concept today, but I've never had any regrets about the sort of discipline that Hockaday gave me." "A passion for thoroughness" was the way a later graduate phrased it. To Miss Hockaday's credit, in an age when women were under no pressure to pursue careers, a surprising number of her graduates gained some national attention as artists, writers, archaeologists, and musicians.

As early as 1935, Miss Hockaday saw fit to bring Judge Sarah T. Hughes to speak to her Junior College students on "A Woman's Opportunities Today." Just what those opportunities were is suggested in these remarks by a student who recorded Judge Hughes' visit in the 1938 Hockaday history:

> *As a result of her talk, my typewriting took on new significance and shorthand was no longer an unintelligible offspring of the Morse code. Later Miss Trent asked her psychology class how many planned careers. Still under the inspiration of Judge Hughes' talk, every hand in the room was raised. The students fully expected a woman like Miss Trent with fifty years of successful teaching behind her to endorse their decision. Instead, she chuckled and said, "I'm sorry; I wanted you all to get married and have children."*

And that is precisely what most of them did. Even many of those Hockaday scholars who showed early promise in their chosen careers willingly exchanged their ambitions for what society regarded as woman's chief service—motherhood and homemaking. Many of them married very well, and as one put it, "never again had the fire in my belly that would have fueled a career."

Hockaday was undoubtedly offering the best education available for women in this region, but, for all its scholars, it is still remembered by most Dallas citizens as a finishing school, "a very adequate education for the gracious life." A private school in those days, by its very nature, was designed to serve a homogeneous segment of the population. Most of the parents Miss Hockaday dealt with knew each other and shared a common purpose in sending their daughters to her school. That is, "Educate my daughter to be a woman of taste who moves gracefully in any social circle. Give us cultured young ladies who will raise the standards of this community by supporting the arts, daughters with a sense of noblesse oblige who feel a responsibility to upgrade this growing city." To that end, Hockaday girls devoted some time to assisting social workers "to make certain that the neediest, most deserving and cleanest families received help" at Christmas. "By these contacts," the 1938 history notes, "the girls saw with heartfelt sympathy and keen interest how the other half lives."

They were also given a thorough grounding in the social graces. Many remember Miss Miriam Morgan, who joined the faculty shortly after the school opened, as the ultimate authority on manners. The Hockaday history even records table manners contests with score cards. Report cards as late as 1948 show that the girls were being graded with an S (Satisfactory) or an I (Improvement Needed) for "knows the meaning of joy" or "speaks in conversational tones" and of course, "behaves in a ladylike manner at all times." "Courtesy caps," green and white beanies, were still being awarded in the sixties.

"Finishing" also meant travel. For nearly a decade between the two world wars, Hockaday sent travel classes abroad. Accounts of these trips are frothy confections of send-off parties at the Waldorf Astoria, orchid corsages, first-class staterooms aboard the *Vulcania,* raucous Spanish sailors in Seville, Christmas in St. Moritz with the Cambridge ski team, tea with Lady Astor, an audience with the pope, the coronation of George VI, Mussolini reviewing his troops in the Villa Borghese, chocolate croissants, and French classes at the Sorbonne. Small wonder that for some women Hockaday was the high point of their lives.

Even those who stayed at home were treated to the museum-quality antique collections of Miss Hockaday's cottage, as well as a steady stream of world-renowned personalities as diverse as concert artist Josef Lhevinne, General Jonathan Wainwright, and later the Reverend Peter Marshall. I am always a little amused when Hockaday graduates point proudly to the visit of Gertrude Stein and her companion Alice B. Toklas in 1935. For one thing, it suggests that Miss Hockaday was willing to suspend her moral imperatives when it came to artistic guests, but I also wonder how many people who met Miss Stein in 1935 had the slightest idea of what she was talking about. "Fusing being with the continuous present?" Indeed. One Junior College student candidly admitted, "Miss Stein was reading from one of her books, a poem concerning 'then' and 'when.' She was very kind, though, and seemed not the least disturbed at our evident lack of understanding of her poems." And what did Gertrude and Alice think of Hockaday? Alice B. Toklas tells us in *The Alice B. Toklas Cookbook:*

> *On to Dallas where we went to stay with Miss Ela Hockaday at her Junior College. It was a fresh new world. Gertrude Stein became attached to the young students, to Miss Hockaday and the life in Miss Hockaday's home and on the campus. . . . The only recipe I carried away was for cornsticks, not knowing in my ignorance that a special iron was required in which to bake them. But when we sailed back to France in my stateroom one was waiting for me, a proof of Miss Hockaday's continuing attentiveness. What did the Ger-*

mans, when they took it in 1944, expect to do with it? And what are they doing with it now?

So what does all of this have to do with Hockaday in 1978? To the casual observer, perhaps very little. In one day I see a dozen or so students sprawled in front of a TV watching *All My Children* in Tarry House, the senior lounge. Mrs. Lively, the executive housekeeper since the early forties, is murmuring that the girls are dropping tangerine seeds in the Great Hall. A blue-jean-clad teacher saunters by on her way to the ceramics studio. A sixth-grade class struggles with computer language—"let" statements, "destructive read-ins," and "content read-outs." The headmaster shakes hands with his students as they enter school for the day and prides himself on knowing most of their names, but for the rest of the day he must concern himself primarily with Hockaday's greatest worry—money. Does Miss Ela live here anymore?

The changes have come gradually. Miss Hockaday, convinced by her "privy council" that her school would never survive estate taxes, agreed in 1942 to transform it into a publicly owned institution operated by a board of trustees. In an emotional letter, she gave the school theoretically to her alumnae. Although she continued to live on the campus, Miss Hockaday officially retired in 1947, just as the second generation was entering Hockaday. She greeted these daughters with the same scrutiny she had given their mothers. One second-generation Hockadaisy recalls her first encounter with Miss Ela. "We had driven in from Amarillo, and my mother saw Miss Hockaday walking across the campus. 'Miss Hockaday, I want you to meet my daughter.' Miss Hockaday took one look at me and said to my mother, 'Oh, Imogene, how could you have allowed this child to dye her eyelashes?' "

Dyed eyelashes were the least of Hockaday's worries in the 1950's. In addition to the second generation, the school was acquiring a new and less restrained constituency—the oil people. Hockaday was becoming a status symbol, to be collected along with oil wells, Neiman's labels, and Cadillacs. Jett Rink's daughters came from the small towns in West Texas and from oil boomtowns in Louisiana and Oklahoma to fill the boarding department at Hockaday. Some of these young girls arrived with special instructions from their parents that the child not be allowed to see any newspapers dealing with her family's fabulous wealth. Others were less discreet. "Somebody was always getting out of class to go donate a building to SMU," recalls one fifties alum. She also recalled that the "oil" girls were likely to be dripping in jewels at the dances and many of them had fancy cars stashed somewhere in town. "Somebody in my class got a Cadillac with a bar in the back for graduation," remembers another. According to these alums, the main recreation for boarding students on Saturday was shopping all day at Neiman Marcus. "I once saw a boarder buy seven vicuña sweaters in one afternoon, just because she was mad at her daddy for sending her away from her boyfriend back home. My mother said, 'Miss Hockaday would never have permitted that.' "

Miss Hockaday died in 1956, and gradually the teachers who had worked closely with her retired or lost their earlier impact. Some of these second-generation daughters had heard so much about Hockaday that by the time they actually enrolled, they were disappointed. "My mother had told me what Miss Grow, the Latin teacher, would say on our first day of class. And she did give the same speech about how you came into this world with only your name . . . and what you do with that name is so important. That may have inspired my mother's generation, but I kept thinking how terrible it was that in all those years Miss Grow had never changed. She said the same words, fought the same Gallic wars, and it never occurred to her that most of us could hardly wait to *change* our names. She was Miss Grow forever, but she wasn't anyone I wanted to emulate. I remember that she spit on the blackboard when she talked facing the board and had to erase the spit. Isn't it awful to remember that? I also remember seeing her squat one day to retrieve a pencil. I was shocked momentarily to see that she had knees just like the rest of us. Unlike my mother, I was a terrible Latin student, so I spent most of the year hearing Miss Grow say, 'Oh, Virginia. I'm so disappointed in you.' "

Like them or not, teachers like Miss Grow had the power to withhold school honors or to vindicate you when you were falsely accused. One alumna recalled being put "on report" for smoking in the rest room. "Miss Grow looked me straight in the eye and said, 'Did you smoke?' Everyone knew you couldn't lie to Miss Grow, so when I said, 'No,' the matter was dropped." Some of these teachers must have been rather like maiden aunts whom you never really liked but who had a disproportionate hold over your life. As another graduate said, "I still have the haunting feeling that because I couldn't live up to Miss Grow's expectations, somewhere it is permanently recorded that I was a failure."

In 1961 Hockaday moved north to a very barren hundred acres on Forest

Lane and Welch Road. The school's original patrons had moved north long before, leaving the gracious gardens of Swiss Avenue and Munger Place in a state of decay. Dallas was growing rapidly and no longer looked to a few families or a school to be the arbiters of taste and culture. Some alumnae reacted violently to the modern edifice on the new campus. One says it still reminds her of a Green Stamp redemption center, and others insist that travelers sometimes mistake it for a motel. The fact is, Hockaday on Welch Road is a *swanky*-looking school. ("Swanky" is a word I'm sure Miss Hockaday never used.) And when someone wants to point a finger at a rich girls' school, Hockaday, with its glassy atrium, is an easy target.

Ironically, this reputation for affluence is one of Hockaday's biggest problems. While it has attracted the daughters of the wealthy, Hockaday has never been a rich school. Miss Hockaday lived from tuition to tuition, charging the groceries and other services until the checks came in. Her teachers were paid minimal wages, especially when you consider the hours they were expected to work overtime chaperoning and supervising. She always had someone like Miss Kribs to see that every square inch of carbon paper was used before a new sheet might be issued. Forty-watt bulbs or less were de rigueur in the hallways of her school, and even Exie Tunson will tell you, "I only worked for a rich lady once. The rest of the time I worked for working people like Miss Hockaday. She sure knew how to cut corners."

"I'm not sure how much longer we can afford the gentility," says the current chairman of the board, Rust Reid. Indeed, Hockaday today is like a very refined lady who has heretofore considered it indiscreet to air financial problems but who has in reality been patching her undergarments for years. Now even Hockaday's outer garments need patching.

The problem is, Hockaday has no funds for the maintenance of the swanky buildings that cost $4 million to build in 1960, but now would cost $12 million to replace. Sure, Hockaday has some generous patrons, but there are few philanthropists who want a bronze plaque on the air-conditioning-repair bill, especially when there are more exciting plans for a gym and a new library on the drawing board.

When Glenn Ballard, the present headmaster, came to Hockaday in 1972, the school had only $130,000 in endowment, which was really designated for faculty retirement benefits. In the past three years, thanks largely to the efforts of Ballard and past chairman of the board Ashley Priddy, the school has been able to raise $3.5 million in donations and pledges. That sounds like a hefty sum until you hear that schools like Andover and Exeter have endowments of $70 million. According to Hockaday's development director, the school needs an endowment of between $10 million and $15 million. Without such an endowment, the school is at the mercy of its donors. For example, Hockaday's library space has been woefully inadequate practically since the building on Welch Road was erected; a recent professional study also showed that the gym facility is now inadequate for Hockaday's comprehensive and growing physical education program. Although the library need has been around longer, in sports-conscious Dallas money to build squash courts, running tracks, and locker rooms is apparently easier to come by these days than money for study carrels.

What motivates people to give to a school like Hockaday? Male institutions can always point to the professional success of their graduates as proof of the school's value. The success of many Hockaday women, beyond college acceptance, may be harder to measure. Some people may give to a school for nostalgic reasons. Even though those Memorial Rooms were expensive to install, Hockaday could not leave them out of its modern structure. There had to be something to tie the alumnae to the new campus.

Although Miss Hockaday was always a forward-looking educator, she could not have conceived of the pressures that would come to bear on her school. The school's constituency has broadened so that there could never be a consensus among parents about what the school should be. The granddaughters of her original graduates are now enrolled. And the second generation of oil money is there. And there seems to be an inordinate number of professional bourgeoisie; one-third of the second-grade class have doctors for fathers. Integration, busing, and experimentation in the public schools have brought still another set of parents to Hockaday. These parents are not necessarily seeking social prestige or Miss Hockaday's ideals; they simply want a safe, decent school in which to park their daughters until the public schools settle down. These are, for the most part, public-educated parents who may have little interest in sending their daughters east to college. In fact, they may be a little distrustful of Hockaday's college counseling. Enrolling her five-year-old daughter in the preschool, one mother actually asked, "Now you're not going to make her marry a Yankee and move away from Dallas, are you?"

In addition to these day students, the school also has a large number of boarding students from South America, as well as an obligatory sprinkling of black students and Mexican Americans. A look at the zip codes in the student directory reveals that Hockaday's day student body converges from all directions. Seventy-eight students come from Highland Park, eight from Oak Cliff, six from the old neighborhood near Greenville, and 249 from the sprawling North Dallas neighborhoods surrounding the school. Still others commute from Garland, Mesquite, Farmers Branch, etc. About all you could safely say these families have in common is the ability to pay the tuition, and quite a few are receiving partial scholarship aid.

While Miss Hockaday and her early faculty members (Miss Trent, Miss Morgan, Miss McDermott) were certainly distinct personalities, they were all unmarried women educators who could and did give their whole lives to the school. Today the faculty and staff at Hockaday are as diverse as the families of the children they serve.

Mrs. Lively, the executive housekeeper, is a lovely Russian lady. She takes me on a tour of the Memorial Rooms and with her charming accent recalls, "How lovely it was! Miss Morgan would ring the bell and the girls would go quietly into the dining room. The tables were set with the linen doilies and nice silverware. The girls, they were so polite. They let their teachers go first. Now," she says with a sigh, "they are not so polite. It is all so fast, you know, *whoosh-whoosh,* in and out. Ah, this cafeteria, Miss Hockaday would not like it. The boarders have a seated dinner only once a week. In the old days it was every night. And there were beautiful flowers and always singing in the Great Hall. Oh, Miss Hockaday loved flowers. I could always find something blooming on the old campus to make a nice centerpiece. Here, if I don't see that the bulbs are planted, no one else will. They don't care so much anymore. There is not time or money for the lovely things anymore."

In stark contrast to Mrs. Lively is Peter Cobb, the new head of the Upper School. Cobb is thirtyish, frizzy-haired, athletically inclined, and certainly handsome enough to provoke a few crushes among his adolescent students. Cobb has a Master of Divinity degree from Union Theological Seminary in New York, where he admits he was something of a radical during the sixties. Coming to Hockaday from the Master's School at Dobbs Ferry, New York, Cobb says, only half-facetiously, "Well, one of the problems we have here is that the girls are too polite." He quickly qualifies his statement by assuring me that he is by no means out to destroy the graciousness of Southern womanhood. As a matter of fact, after his years on the East Coast, he's rather taken by it. But he feels the school has a tremendous responsibility to prepare girls for careers that may demand aggressiveness, initiative, and a willingness to take risks. I couldn't help smiling at the irony of Hockaday's teaching girls to take risks when so many of their parents sent them there to be safe.

It is also curious that Miss Hockaday herself must have successfully blended the aggressiveness and graciousness in her career, but when she retired, she chose a man, Hobart Mossman, to succeed her. Indeed, for all of its talk about limitless opportunities for women, Hockaday has not had a headmistress since Miss Hockaday. For that matter, with the exceptions of the foreign language and physical education departments, which have no male teachers, all of the Upper School departments are headed by men.

I also asked Glenn Ballard, Hockaday's personable headmaster, about possible conflicts in trying to produce professionally successful young women in a Southern girls' school. Headmasters of private schools are inevitably able public relations men, and any reporter has a tendency to discount their statements as boosterism. Nevertheless, Ballard says the broadening of Hockaday's constituency has helped provide profession-bound girls with models to emulate. "The mothers of Hockaday students now run the gamut from those who wear white gloves and go to tea parties or luncheons every day to moms who have retained their maiden names and have careers of their own. The mothers, on the whole, have a better grasp of what it is we're trying to do and they are for the most part supportive. The fathers tend to relish their daughters' growing independence, but experience more ambivalent feelings. Occasionally a father admits that he wishes she'd just imitate her mother." Both Cobb and Ballard insist that they find working in a girls' school so satisfying that they never long for a night out with the boys.

The faculty, like any contemporary school faculty, can be broken down into three or four types. There are the teachers who basically like kids and who never count the hours they spend counseling with them after school. There are the serious scholars who enjoy the students who share their passion for a particular subject. And perhaps at schools like Hockaday there are some who stick around primarily because they enjoy the prestige of association with prominent parents. How about a parent conference with Braniff president Harding Lawrence and his ad executive wife, Mary Wells? And, as at any school, there are the older faculty members who tend to believe that they are the only ones doing any real teaching. They lament the fact that their classes seem to be something to occupy students' time between extracurricular activities.

Some recall sweeter days when the cultural vibrations went from Dallas homes to the school. One teacher remembers days when parents had poets or musicians visiting in their homes and would agree to share their friends with the school. "Now," he says, "it seems to be the other way around. The intellectual climate in Hockaday homes is not what it used to be." This spring, a Broadway musical performance seemed to be causing a bit of rancor among teachers and parents. One parent complained, "I was glad my daughter was chosen to be in *Mame,* but after the time she spent on rehearsals, I began to wonder, 'Did I send her to Hockaday to learn to be a Las Vegas showgirl?' "

Some of the younger faculty members seem to be imbued with a frontier spirit. Teaching in a girls' school is no longer a second-class job. Hockaday is sending girls to Stanford, Princeton, Yale, Harvard, Rice, and MIT. The curriculum is demanding, and the faculty seems increasingly distinguished academically. Nobody teaches at Hockaday for the money. Salaries range from $19,000 for a beginning teacher to $21,000 for a department head, plus grants for summer graduate work. Nevertheless, teaching at Hockaday is a luxury, especially if you've ever taught in a public school. The girls are rather easily motivated, and the small class sizes make the teacher-pupil relationship potentially very rewarding. "Where else," says Dean of Faculty Dr. Tezzie Cox, "could we read ten Shakespeare plays in one year and write papers on each of them?" Private school teaching can provide all of the stimulation of teaching at the college level without any of the headaches of "publish or perish."

But there are also awesome responsibilities and pressures in teaching at Hockaday. There is the ego involvement of successful, upwardly mobile parents who want to believe that Hockaday can work miracles. "They pay for it," says a faculty member, "so by golly, you figure out a way to get their baby through. If she can't handle the curriculum you've set up, then you change it." Parents are also concerned about Hockaday's maintaining traditional standards in the face of grade inflation everywhere else. "I sent my daughter to Hockaday because it is a college preparatory school," says one parent, "and the irony of it is that the C she's making in a Hockaday English class, where no grade higher than C is being given, will probably knock her chances for the college of her choice."

What is it like to be a student at Hockaday? Some girls will spend fourteen school years there. Hockaday recently added a preschool for four-year-olds, and since many people seem to believe that once you're in, you're in for good, there is considerable competition even at that early age. Miss

Hockaday used to interview each prospective student personally. Now an admissions office handles the interviews. "When I interviewed at Hockaday for the seventh grade, I remember being asked what college I planned to attend. I think I said Smith because that's where my mother went," one graduate recalls. The pressure is on.

Most of these girls are the daughters of achievers and they know that their parents have high expectations. As one Lower School teacher put it, "I sometimes worry that these little girls never get to do something just for the fun of it. Their lives are so programmed. They take piano lessons, gymnastics, go to choir practice, get tutored in math or reading, or go to ballet. By the ninth grade or even earlier, they are worrying about college acceptance. They are told that good grades alone will not assure them of admission to a prestige college. So now they must spend their summers 'productively,' teaching deaf kids, going to Andover summer school, or learning photography—anything that will make them an 'attractive package' when their application crosses the college admissions desk. It seems as if they are always living their lives in preparation for the next hurdle. Some are even taught to be socially calculating at a very early age. I worry that they never get the chance to just be—to just lie in the sun and let the wind tickle their toes. It may sound like heresy, but I think a little benign neglect might be healthy for some of them."

What do Hockaday girls look like? They're mostly green and white, and beyond seventh grade have waist-length blond hair, gold ear studs, and saddle oxfords, and they wear their green sweaters tied around their waists. When I asked several of them what misconceptions they thought most people had about Hockaday, they responded, "Tell them that we're not all just a bunch of rich girls." "And we're not a bunch of lesbians, either," giggled another. The green and white uniforms do go a long way toward concealing any economic differences in the student body, but as one recent graduate told me, "Aw, everybody knows who's got money and who doesn't. Look at the parking lot. You know who drives the Mark IV with 'Molly-16' on the license plate." And there are subtle ways of distinguishing yourself even in a uniform—Gucci key rings and Rolex watches. One alum remarked, "I wouldn't mind being black or brown or green at Hockaday; I'd just hate to be poor."

After being at Hockaday for a few days, I think I'd mainly hate to be stupid. I talked with the mother of a Mexican American student who is certainly, by Hockaday standards, "less well-off." She did not feel that her daughter had suffered any discrimination at Hockaday. "She knows who she is. She doesn't try to compete socially, and quite frankly she finds the activities of some of her very affluent classmates rather entertaining. Although there is certainly competition at Hockaday for grades and in athletics, there also seems to be some very healthy pride in each other's achievements. My daughter won an award and found her locker decorated with ribbons and notes of congratulations. She really appreciates that esprit de corps." In all fairness, it should be noted that this particular student is also one of the brightest kids at Hockaday. Her mother did go on to say that she was also pleased to hear Peter Cobb talking to parents about the girls' need to develop life skills. ("They can program a computer, but can they put the chain back on their bikes?" he once asked.) "I wanted to tell the parents that their kids could develop a lot of life skills if they would just unplug their maids," this working mother said. "Like a lot of Hockaday parents, I complain about the amount of homework, but I'm complaining for a different reason. I need her to help with the housework at night."

You can't sit in classes at Hockaday or even walk down the halls—which are filled with art exhibits, interesting book displays, and the sound of a voice student rehearsing her recital in the Great Hall—without worrying that education is wasted on the young. One recent graduate told me that she remembers walking into the building for her admissions interview: "I thought, 'This is all so fantastic, but I'll bet someday I take it all for granted.' And I did." No matter how splendid the educational atmosphere may be, kids are kids, and their immaturity will always limit what they can absorb. "We always spent more time figuring out how we could sneak out of the symphony performance at McFarlin Auditorium to get ice cream on the SMU drag than we did listening to the symphony," recalls one graduate of the fifties.

I sat through an English class in the Upper School, where students were analyzing Hemingway's story "The Killers." The insightful reading they had apparently given their homework assignment was remarkable. Another class was reading John Knowles' *A Separate Peace,* a novel with built-in appeal for Hockaday girls since the story deals with a boys' boarding school. As they read, the students kept critical journals that facilitated reference to imagery and recurring themes. When the class was over, I had to stifle an impulse to shake each little girl and say, "Do you have any idea how lucky you are? You won't get this sort of teaching and individual attention until you get to graduate school, if then." Few classes in Hockaday's

Upper School exceed fifteen students. Some have only nine. You can't get lost in the crowd.

Some complain, however, that though you may not get lost, you can certainly be overlooked when the awards are handed out. Some kids thrive on the competition and the pressure of such an environment. Miss Hockaday herself was a great believer in pushing girls to achieve their highest potential. But there are so many more distractions today and so many more areas in which girls can achieve. One parent said, "I couldn't be happier with Hockaday; my only concern is that my daughter feels compelled to be a Renaissance woman, and she may burn out trying to be the best in everything."

I heard a lot of talk about "burning out" from parents who are concerned about their ambitious daughters. Although some of the girls are quite certain about their chosen careers, there are still plenty of kids who don't feel entirely secure with the liberation that has been thrust upon them. For some, their primary concern may still be "Somebody show me how to care what men think." "My daughter tells people she's going to be a nurse just because she feels she has to have some career plan in mind, but I think all she knows about herself at this point is that she likes to sing," said one mother. The younger students at Hockaday may not suffer this loss of confidence when they're seniors because they will have had a longer time to contemplate the opportunities. I am told that there is a four-foot-tall seventh grader at Hockaday who is certain that she will cure cancer. Others in the lower grades speak glibly of spending a few years at Time-Life before launching brilliant literary careers. It makes you wonder who's going to run the charity balls and arts benefit auctions of the future.

What would Miss Hockaday have to say about all of this? She might find a lot of it "highly irregular," but then again, I think she might also see threads of continuity that would be pleasing to her. In addition to the excellent sports training that Hockaday has always given, the school still fosters a love of reading. My contemporaries who graduated from Hockaday in the early sixties are among the best-read women I know, and I think Hockaday had something to do with it. And as any girls' school must, Hockaday appreciates female wit—particularly wit with some intellectual sophistication. So if these ambitious graduates should opt for the gracious life some of their mothers have led, they won't be entirely unequipped.

Very little of Hockaday's finishing school tradition still exists. However, I did sit in on a Form meeting in the Upper School and hear a debate over who should be honored at their tea. Even in 1978, hardly anyone graduates without having properly poured tea at least once during her high school years. And Miss Hockaday's belief that her girls should be exposed to outstanding personalities continues. In recent years Hockaday girls have talked informally with Gloria Steinem, Nancy Dickerson, Lily Kraus, Nobel prizewinner Norman E. Borlaug, and a host of artists, poets, and authors of children's books. These extraordinary experiences are served up so frequently that I occasionally wonder if life after Hockaday will seem dreadfully dull.

Miss Hockaday would feel completely comfortable with graduation. Except that there is no pergola on the new campus, graduation is unchanged. Lower School girls dressed in white are first in the procession arranged by class and according to height. Sisters of the graduates still form an honor guard arch of gladiolas through which the entire procession passes. The seniors, wearing long white dresses that have been supplied by Neiman Marcus since 1916 and broad-brimmed pastel horsehair hats (now purchased at Kmart if you're on a tight budget) and carrying wicker baskets of fresh-cut flowers, proceed in measured, much-practiced steps to "Land of Hope and Glory" and take their seats in the bleachers in front of the assembled parents and guests. The speaker this year is Dr. Hanna Holborn Gray, new president of the University of Chicago. Eleanor Roosevelt gave the commencement address in 1952. The student body still sings "O Brother Man" and concludes with a tearful "Taps" as the flag is lowered. In 1970 there was a brief struggle to include "Bridge Over Troubled Water," but tradition won out.

Tradition has a strong hold on Hockaday. The alumnae took Miss Hockaday seriously when she wrote: "And my dear ones, I know you will care for and nourish this school of yours and mine through the years to come." As I wrote this article, people kept insisting that I compare Hockaday with St. Mark's. One parent summed it up neatly when she admitted that all of the clamoring for Hockaday to be like St. Mark's was rather like Henry Higgins' soliloquy for *My Fair Lady:* "Why can't a woman be more like a man?" Because of its longer history and because it is in the business of educating girls, Hockaday is a far more complex school. For many of its alumnae, it was not just a school; it was a way of looking at life. "St. Mark's," as headmaster Ted Whatley will tell you, "is a Sputnik school pragmatically established by industrialists who were interested in turning out scientists."

It also occurred to me that men seem to pass through the institutions of their youth—schools, camps, fraternities—and if these are pleasant, worthwhile experiences, they may send occasional checks or letters of recommendation for a friend's child. Women, on the other hand, tend to be more sentimental about their institutions. Perhaps we also view ourselves as custodians of important traditions that men might ignore. Or perhaps because so few of us pursued careers until recently, we have stronger feelings about our high school and college days as days of important achievement. At any rate, the fact is, women have traditionally had the time to remain involved with their institutions. As one "outsider" put it, "Hockaday seems to be both a victim and a beneficiary of its own success. It graduated all of these intelligent, strong, concerned, opinionated women and now they return full force with their daughters and all sorts of ideas as to how the school should be run."

Sometimes the alumnae may be too caught up in preserving the past. One board member recalls making an impassioned plea for the upgrading of the science library at Hockaday. To illustrate his point, he passed out some very dated science books that were still in the Hockaday library. When he sat down, a white-gloved hand went up. "You know, you're absolutely right about the library, and I think the first thing we should do is get these books of Miss Hockaday's bound in leather."

Hockaday will not be able to shake its "rich" reputation because it has very affluent alumnae, who, like the school's founder, have an uncompromising demand for quality in their lives—only the best will do. For some, that means being sure that the cafeteria still serves excellent food or arranging for the Latin Banquet to be held at Brook Hollow Golf Club. For others, it may mean giving a lovely silver tureen to be used at tea parties or an exquisite rug for a Memorial Room. A display case in the hall arranged by alumnae last week featured the 1923 Idlewild Ball gown, slippers, and dance program of dear Miss Louise Kribs, the bookroom bulldog who frightened me so eight years ago. These small, cozy gestures seem to say, "You may educate our daughters for the future, but we will not let you forget who you once were."

But some of the alumnae are concerned with more than the quality of the material things that surround Hockaday. These are the women with the liberal arts educations who feel that Hockaday gave them a self-reliance that grew out of knowing some things thoroughly. They worry that as the school has grown, broadened its aims, and offered more options to accommodate more tastes, it is in danger of losing the vision and cohesiveness that it had in the early days. They worry that the school will founder in trying to be all things to all people. They are skeptical of current trends that say, "Establish your career goals and we will shape the education for them."

These are the crosscurrents and paradoxes that are Hockaday today. The school is rich and poor; it is new and also old; shiny glass buildings house elegant antique-filled rooms; girls wear streamlined uniforms and carry calculators, but the same girls will also don horsehair hats and pour tea.

Mrs. Lively, the housekeeper, eyes me suspiciously as I have coffee in one of the Memorial Rooms with a young staff member. There is a classic standoff here between the generations, and I am in the middle. Like the watchful eye of a curator in a museum, Mrs. Lively's look implies, "This is all we have of her lovely things and they must be preserved, so drink your coffee elsewhere." And the younger generation stubbornly ignores her reproving glance and finishes her coffee as if to say, "The past is lovely, but when it ceases to be useful in the present, how can we justify the cost of maintaining it?" I am uncomfortably in between, still pragmatically using Grandmother's hollow-handle knives but polishing them more often and no longer tossing them into the dishwasher. I think Hockaday is too.

Sisterhood Is Powerful

OF ALL THE TRAPPINGS of my four years at the University of Texas, only one followed me to Dallas and appears destined to be with me the rest of my life: my sorority. Maligned and revered, the butt of jokes and jibes and the goal of countless anxious mothers for their daughters, sororities have kept their place in the rites of passage of a whole segment of Texas society that moves from summer camp to sorority to Junior League, with the same basic rituals serving at each level to strengthen the bond of women together. When I returned to Austin last fall to witness sorority rush, I had expected that the intervening years of the late sixties and the seventies would have changed things utterly. Instead, I found my memories going back to my own rush.

It was the fall of 1962, and I had just hobbled in ill-fitting stiletto-heeled shoes from the Chi Omega house on Wichita to the Tri Delt house on Twenty-seventh Street in Austin. Word had not reached Texarkana that during rush week, regardless of the University policy that forbade freshmen to have cars, it was unseemly to walk from sorority house to sorority house. Socially astute and ambitious mothers from Houston and Dallas had willingly stranded themselves at the Villa Capri motel near campus, so that their daughters could drive the family car and arrive poised and oblivious to the beastly Austin September sun in their de rigueur dark cottons.

My dark cottons were severely circled under the armpits and the humidity made me regret the tight permanent wave that my mother had felt was necessary to keep my already naturally curly hair out of my eyes. The lengthy walk had made me late, and I half hoped that I could sit this one out. But before I could blot the sweat from my upper lip, a vivacious girl costumed like Judy Garland's dog, Toto, pinned a huge name tag on me and led me down a cardboard yellow brick road into the cool interior of her sorority house.

Like young Jay Gatsby, I had seldom been in such beautiful houses before. Although F. Scott Fitzgerald never mentioned Daisy's sorority affiliation, these houses—particularly the Tri Delt and Pi Phi houses—could have been hers. Like Gatsby, I suspected that these houses held "ripe mystery . . . a hint of bedrooms upstairs more beautiful and cool than other bedrooms, of gay and radiant activities taking place through its corridors." I was much too naive to recognize voices "full of money," but I did marvel at the inexhaustible charm of these breathless beauties. I wrote to my parents after that first day of parties with Pi Phis, Tri Delts, Zetas, Chi Omegas, Kappas, and Thetas that I had never seen such a gathering of beautiful girls in my life. "High in a white palace, the king's daughters, the golden girls"—in Pappagallo shoes.

Sororities at the University of Texas in 1962 were large by national standards. If all pledges remained active, a UT sorority could usually boast close to 150 active members. Even if only half of them were really beauties, the effect was overwhelming when you saw them—exquisitely groomed—in one large room.

After what seemed interminable non-conversation and punch that never really quenched one's thirst, the lights dimmed at the Tri Delt house, and Toto gave me a quick squeeze. "You just sit right here on the front row. I'll be back when the skit is over." My naiveté once again kept me from being impressed by this privileged front-row position. Being squired around by a costumed sorority personality, I would later learn, also might indicate favoritism. The skits blur a little in my mind, but they were nothing less than major musical productions, often with professional lighting and costumes. We were the tail end of a generation raised on Broadway musicals and consequently were prime suckers for lyrics lifted from *Carousel* or *South Pacific* and altered for sorority purposes. I distinctly remember a green-eyed Tri Delt named Kay dressed as the carnival barker from *Carousel* sending shivers down my spine with "When you walk through a storm, hold your head up high . . ." It was that unflinching eye contact that got me every time, and by the end of the week, if you were a desirable rushee, someone might be squeezing your elbow by the time Kay's voice reached the final "You'll never walk aaalone." Although the songs varied, that was the pitch at most of the houses. The girls locked arms around the room and swayed gently as they sang, all to remind you that it was a big University and that joining these self-confident beauties meant not having to face it alone.

As I watched these sorority girls flash their perfect teeth and sing and dance, I surmised that they possessed secrets that they might share if I managed to get out of the foyer and into those upstairs rooms. They not only knew their way to class on the 150 acres that then composed the University, but they also knew appropriate retorts when drunk Kappa Sigs pulled their skirts up at parties and howled, "Look at the wheels on this woman!" I knew they could hold their beer and their cool when someone "dropped trou" or toga at a Fiji Island party. I was sure that they did not worry—as I did—about where one slept when one accepted an OU-Texas date to Dallas or when one made the bacchanalian pilgrimage to Laredo for George Washington's Birthday.

But the week was not all costumed escorts, squeezes, and front-row seats. Sometimes the carefully concealed rush machinery broke down and the party lost its air of graciousness. A survivor recalls that in the grand finale of the *Carousel* skit, performers tossed bags of popcorn to prize rushees on the front row. One player overshot the front row, but remedied her error by wrenching the popcorn bag from the second-row innocent's hand and restoring it to its intended mark. More often the embarrassing moments were brought on by a provincial rushee. It's probably apocryphal, but the story floated around for years that, on being passed a silver tray of cigarettes, a rushee at the Zeta house looked puzzled for a moment, then reached furtively into her purse, emptied her cigarette pack onto the tray, and quickly passed it on.

At the Pi Phi house I once held four "floaters" (sorority members who moved in and out of many circles at each party to get an overall picture of the rushees) captive with a fifteen-minute maudlin tale about the day my dog died when I was eleven. They feigned intense interest, their eyes brimming at appropriate times, but doubtless they collapsed in spasms of laughter and goose calls when I made my exit. The next day, to my horror, I was repeatedly introduced at the Pi Phi house with, "This is Prudence. Get her to tell you that neat story about her dog."

But despite our faux pas, my roommates and I had an easy time of it. We were under no parental pressure to pledge at all. Totally ignorant of the machinations of rush, we innocently perceived the whole rush week scene as one exhausting and bewildering but happy experience in which we were to decide whom we liked best. We had only the vaguest notions about sorority rankings on campus. Although there were twenty sororities on the UT campus in 1962, for many girls, accepting a bid from other than the "big six" was apparently unthinkable. We were aware of tears down the hall as "cuts" were made by the sororities following the first and second periods of parties, but we could not appreciate the pain of the "legacy" (the daughter of a sorority alum) whose mother responded to her daughter's rejection with, "Pack your bags, honey. SMU has deferred rush." Or the one who declared, "See, I told you you should have gone to Tech first"—where it was easier to make it into an elite sorority and then transfer to UT.

The third period of rush week consisted of two Saturday evening parties. It was tense, and girls on both sides were exhausted. Members had culled their rushee lists to approximately 100. Too many rushees at a final-period party could scare top rushees away. ("There were ten Houston girls at that party; they won't take us all.") In 1962 rushees were required to wear "after five" dresses to these parties. Members usually dressed in white or, in the case of the Kappas, in sepulchral black. Sidewalks were lined with hurricane lamps and the houses were candlelit. This was the party for sentimental tearjerkers. The Thetas were renowned for leaving no dry eyes. The Tri Delts put a string of pearls around your neck and instructed you to toss a wishing pearl in a shell fountain while an alumna with a haunting voice sang mysteriously from an upstairs window. The Kappas still croon in four-part harmony.

And when we tell you
How wonderful you are,
You'll never believe it.
You'll never believe it.
That girls so fine could ever be
united in fraternity
And they all wear the little golden key.
[descant: ah-ah-ah-ah]
And when you wear one,
And you're certainly going to wear one.

[This is when the not-so-subtle
elbow squeeze came.]
The proudest girl in this wide world
you'll be
You'll never believe it.
You'll never believe it.
That from this great wide world
We've chosen YOU.
[Really look 'em in the eye.]

After two such parties (a first and second preference), the rushees departed for Hogg Auditorium to sign preference cards, which would be sorted by computer. Needless to say, no one folded, spindled, or mutilated her card. Sorority members would be up in all-night final hash sessions to determine their top fifty choices. On Sunday afternoon, the computer would print out the results. Panhellenic representatives sat with boxes of alphabetized envelopes. For appearances' sake, there was an envelope for every girl who had attended a final party, but some contained cards with the message, "You have received no sorority bid at this time. Please feel free to come by the Panhellenic office to register for open rush." Amid the squealing and squeezing that went on as envelopes were ripped open, perhaps it was possible to run unnoticed from the room with such an envelope and back to a lonely dorm room for a bitter cry. We were among the shriekers and squeezers and we did not notice. My three roommates and I had received bids to the same sorority, and our course was set.

Although we were to become somewhat aberrant sorority members, we had unwittingly chosen our bridesmaids, the godmothers for our future children, and access to certain social circles. Others in our pledge class already had this social entrée by virtue of their birth; numerous legacies recall hearing Kappa songs as lullabies. I remember being fascinated by a framed family tree that hung in the study hall of the Kappa house. The genealogy was illustrated by linking Kappa keys (the sorority symbol) indicating that all of the women in this family had been Kappas for four generations. I distinctly remember feeling sorry for these girls whose choices were made inevitable by long family tradition. Still others had simply been born in the right neighborhoods and had distinguished themselves in the privileged big-city high schools—which then were Lamar (Houston), Alamo Heights (San Antonio), Highland Park (Dallas), and Arlington Heights (Fort Worth).

Small-town sorority members might have already joined these elite circles at expensive summer camps. Only one of my new Kappa roommates had done any of these things. She was a product of Camp Mystic, had attended a boarding school, recognized prestige clothing labels, and generally knew her way around the social scene into which the other three of us had stumbled. She was appalled at our ignorance. We had blindly selected our sorority because we liked each other and because we agreed that the Kappas' whole rush setup was pleasantly amateurish and not at all intimidating. Quite frankly, we felt like we might be able to help them out. In a small-town high school, where rivalry was not particularly fierce, one tended to get an inflated idea of one's abilities and talents. In a competitive big-city high school, one might be a cheerleader or serve on the student council, but in a smaller pond like ours, it was entirely possible to be cheerleader, star in the senior play, be the editor of the school paper, participate as a member, and probably an officer, in every school organization, and still do well scholastically.

When we expressed these reasons for pledging later in a rush evaluation questionnaire, our active "sisters," knowing that our egos could obviously take it, were quick to inform us that our pledge class had been a tremendous disappointment.

There were other illusions destroyed that freshman year. Girls who had chastely sung of truth, beauty, and honor during rush and had even lectured our pledge class on ladylike behavior befitting a sorority member would be seen holding forth with sloshing beer cup atop the toilet seat in the powder room during a Sigma Chi match party, "Furthermore, remember, you *can* drink like a lady."

But the scales would not really drop from our eyes until rush the following year. We had spent many summer hours rewriting and casting skits and painting new scenery, and though exhausted, we looked forward to being on the other side of rush with the enthusiasm that only one who has not already endured it can possess. The business of UT rush was mind-boggling. Every member was required to attend unless she was out of the country. On arrival in Austin the week before rush week, members were handed a schedule of workshop activities and a list of at least 300 names with pertinent information about each rushee. Hours and hours were spent in the basement with a slide projector flashing pictures of rushees on a screen while we shouted names, hometowns, and other key facts. I was totally unprepared for the power blocs from the big cities. Houston might send twenty highly recommended girls through our rush, but the actives from Houston already knew which ones were to be eliminated before the end of the week. Gradually, as the pictures became more familiar on the screen during the workshop, someone would shout out in the darkened room, "Gotta get that girl!" or "Key to Houston—get her, we get 'em all" or "Theta legacy–Theta pledge, forget her." As the sessions got longer, girls became giddy and pictures of less-than-beautiful girls would be greeted with uncharitable mooing. I learned to become exceedingly wary of those airbrushed Neiman Marcus/Gittings portraits of girls in their Hockaday graduation gowns.

Besides giving us some sight recognition of the rushees, I think "the flicks," as we called the grueling picture sessions in the basement, served another purpose. When combined with song memorizing, skit practices, loss of sleep, and evangelical exhortations to "Fire up!" they produced a certain single-mindedness that would enable almost-grown women to revert to what in retrospect seems incredibly childish behavior. Happenings in the outside world had no bearing on our lives that week. What really mattered was stealing Houston's adorable Jo Frances Tyng away from the Pi Phis. By the end of rush week, when all but the diehards had conceded loss, we dubbed her "Ring-ching-Tyng" (as in "Ring-ching Pi Beta Phi," a song sung to the jingle of gold charm bracelets at the Pi Phi house).

"Silence rules" prescribed by Panhellenic to prevent undue pressure on any rushee only contributed to the unreality of the whole experience. From the time they arrived in Austin until the end of rush week, rushees could associate only with other rushees. They could not have dates or talk to their parents. Sorority members were isolated in their respective houses with all telephones disconnected except one. Such isolation on both sides set the scene for considerable emotional buildup, hence the tears by third-period party, which were variously interpreted as "she loves us—we've got her" or "she loves us, but her mother was a Zeta and called her, crying." In retrospect, I think all the tears were small nervous breakdowns.

When rush week began that year, we poured through the front door clapping and yelling, "I'm a Kappa Gamma, awful glad I amma, a rootin-tootin' K-K-G." I remember being slightly embarrassed by the peculiar stares we received from nonparticipants passing by, but nevertheless I sought out my assigned rushee and did my best to "give her a good rush" (introduce her to as many people as I could). By the third party of the day, our mouths were so dry that we sometimes had trouble getting our lips down over our teeth when the perpetual rush smile was no longer required. I was chastised more than once by a rush captain who saw me monopolize a rushee by having some "meaningful conversation" with her away from the babbling crowds, thus spoiling her chances for maximum recognition in the cut session that night.

The language of rush week almost requires a special lexicon. After the first round of parties, I was bewildered by the basement voting sessions. The rush captain had to keep things moving and be sure that sufficient people were dropped from our list each night to keep subsequent parties from being overcrowded. Certain signals developed for the sake of expediency. Members in agreement with a favorable comment being made on a rushee would begin to snap their fingers. Widespread finger snapping meant the rushee had sufficient support and that discussion could be curtailed. I also encountered that wonderful euphemism "the courtesy cut." The rush captain carefully explained that we owed it to legacies to cut them after first-period parties if we did not intend to pledge them. "That way they can go another direction," she reasoned with us. We never allowed ourselves to consider that other houses were cutting the girl that night because she was *our* legacy—leaving her *no* "direction" to go. To avoid gossipy invasions of a rushee's past indiscretions, any doubts about a girl's reputation were phrased, "I don't believe she is Kappa material." From a reasonably credible source, this phrase could utterly destroy the rushee's chances—no further discussion needed. Another shorthand signal that either cut a rushee from the list or initiated a lengthy debate was, "Y'all, I just think she'd be happier elsewhere." I remember one particularly stormy evening when this phrase was used on an active member's sister.

It took me until the second year of rush to perceive the battle lines that inevitably were drawn within chapters during rush. We dubbed it "the flowers versus the flowerpots." One ludicrous evening the debate in the basement had gone hot and heavy over a girl who had outstanding recommendations, scholastic average, activity record, and family background. She simply wasn't "beautiful, adorable, and precious." Just as the fingers began to snap favorably, a member whom I recall as being particularly nonproductive except during rush, gained the floor and whined, as only Texas girls can, "But yew-all, would you ask your boyfriend to get her a date?" The strongest proponent of the girl rose to her feet and shouted, "We've got enough flowers in this chapter! What we need are some pots to put them in." My sentiments were usually with the pots, the solid citizens who kept the chapter machinery rolling by doing the undesirable jobs, kept the grade-point average high, and generally provided the diversity and good humor that flowers who rose at 5:30 a.m. to begin teasing and spraying their hair so often lacked. Flowers, of course, performed the essential function of keeping the sorority's reputation with fraternities high enough to ensure a steady stream of eligible males in and out the front door.

Although alumnae money and time kept the sorority houses well furnished, alumnae pressure varied from house to house. During rush week only one alum adviser was allowed at voting sessions, but alumnae could attend the parties. Aside from the pressure they exerted in the cities as to who received recommendations, alums had little influence in our rush. Friends from other sororities say that they were constantly plagued with alumnae who could not resist offering unauthorized "oral bids" at their parties. The Thetas, in those days, were traditionally beset by alumnae, not only from Austin but also from Houston and Dallas. Making an impression on Mrs. Alum at a party might be just as important as being labeled "precious" by the entire Houston active contingent. One former rush captain recalled a very persistent alum who as a last resort threatened to keep all the active members from her hometown out of the Junior League if they didn't see to it that a certain legacy was pledged. The girl was pledged, but regrettably her pledge pin was jerked before the year was out for swimming nude with a dozen boys at their fraternity house after curfew.

At the end of the week the final vote was taken. The final usually included about three-fourths flowers and one-fourth pots, with legacies who had survived the courtesy cuts securely listed at the top. Other names could be shifted around in the last-minute voting session held after the tearful final-preference party. This was the party where oral bids, strictly prohibited by Panhellenic, slipped out. Rushees hoping for some assurance or just overcome by emotion would weep and hug their active friends at the end of the party and say, "Oh, I just wish I could stay here forever." Statements like these would cause an uproar in the downstairs sessions. A cynic would rise and say, "Yeah, she said the same thing to the Pi Phis an hour ago." But a believer would respond, "Y'all, I know she has a Pi Phi mother and two active sisters, but she wants us . . . I know she does. We've got to move her up the list."

The computer had its final say, and by Sunday afternoon, since several sororities were fiercely competing for the same fifty girls, everyone's list had been altered somewhat. New pledges were greeted once again with hugging and squealing and after a quick supper were lined up like so many prize cattle in an auction to be inspected by the ultimate judges—the fraternity men. One of my favorite flowerpots recalled it this way. "If you were a beauty, you were immediately asked for a date and taken out of the gruesome inspection line. Because we were arranged alphabetically, I got to stand next to someone named Tancy, five-feet-two, curvy, giggly . . . well, precious. Ten minutes after we lined up, she was surrounded with guys elbowing and shoving to get closer. I was ignored unless someone needed to know Tancy's name. I vividly remember standing there, awkward and skinny, alternately wishing painful and exotic diseases on Tancy and at the same time cursing my parents for spending all that money on my 'intellectual development' instead of taking me to a good plastic surgeon in Dallas. I felt a little guilty when cute little Tancy was pregnant by December and had to depledge."

Pledges were guaranteed a date every night during University registration week, thanks to the efforts of fraternity and sorority social chairmen who laboriously matched girl pledge class with boy pledge class and posted the lists at the respective houses. At least two of my "match" dates took one look at my name and were suddenly called away to their grandmothers' funerals. It was just as well; I could never drink enough beer to get into the swing of fraternity parties anyway. Even after I became an active member, no one ever shared the secrets of the cool retort and, sure enough, tears came to my eyes when a drunk Kappa Sig pulled my dress up in the middle of the dance floor. I often wonder if some of my contemporaries who married their fraternity boyfriends, and have since divorced, perhaps mistook three years of standing arm in arm, with sloshing beer cups, in front of blaring bands as real intimacy. Could it be that when the keg stopped flowing and the music quit playing, they found they hardly knew each other?

Within the sorority system, however, good friendships did develop. Perhaps we would have experienced the same bonding in a dorm or co-op; however, I doubt that I would have known 150 women on the University campus as well as I did these without such a formal structure.

My sorority sisters and I did serve at each other's weddings, and my children *do* have a Kappa godmother. We still exchange the Christmas cards with the long notes attached. Although we were frequently stereotyped as "look-alike-think-alikes" by our critics, within a group of 150 girls there was inevitable diversity. These were the days when the Bored Martyrs (a notorious women's drinking society) were witty girls who truly could have been Mortar Boards (an honor society) if they hadn't become cynical so young. We also had our share of philosophy majors, musicians, artists whose rooms were boycotted by the maids and labeled fire hazards by the fire marshal, campus politicians, professional bridge players, and party girls who frequently majored in elementary education or jumped from college to college fleeing scholastic probation. Most were, of course, from wealthy families, and for me, who had attended a high school where only 15 percent of the graduates went on to college, it was an education in how the other half lived. I'll never forget my father's first visit to the Kappa house. He stood in the foyer gazing at the lovely furnishings and curved stairway. "Honey," he said, "why do you bother to come home?" The sorority parking lot was filled with the latest-model automobiles; one sister drove a classy vintage Mercedes. When a fire damaged the Dallas Neiman Marcus one fall, there was genuine distress over whether Christmas would come that year. Being a part of the Greek community in the early sixties was a way of feeling rooted in the state. These were privileged little girls, and their daddies and some of their mothers were powerful people—University regents, renowned doctors, influential lawyers, judges, kingmakers, or politicians themselves. The young fraternity men we dated became lawyers, doctors, bankers, went into "investments," or joined their fathers' successful businesses. In the course of an afternoon spent doing volunteer work in Parkland Hospital's emergency room recently, I heard the names of three blind dates from my freshman year being paged as resident doctors. Texas Law Review banquets and Bar conventions are like homecomings, where the men still greet the women with the standard fraternity embrace. Even after fourteen years, the wives, especially the Houston flowers, are still quite glamorous. Flowerpots are more scattered, as they frequently pursued careers that took them out of the South. One writes from New York as an assistant editor of a magazine, "Remember, I may have been a late bloomer—but I bloomed!" Others have become artists, lawyers, biologists, or academicians at universities where sororities are once again on the upswing. "I was invited with five other faculty members to a sorority house recently for what I think we called apple-polishing night," writes one who is now an English professor. "After dinner the girls sang to us. The four male profs looked delighted, but I couldn't resist searching the crowd to discern the pots from the flowers."

With such continuity of friendship, social education, and broad acquaintance across the state, I can hardly dismiss my sorority experience. By the time we reached our junior year in college, however, many of us had begun to sense that something was amiss. There were strong conflicts between belonging to a sorority and trying to pursue an education. Why did we volunteer our time to help the Phi Delts gather wood for the Aggie bonfire when I could have been with my English class buddies hearing Tom Wolfe and Truman Capote? I missed Igor Stravinsky's visit to campus because I was the song leader at chapter dinner. In retrospect, the conflict was most apparent when the sorority pretended to serve academic purposes. The poet John Crowe Ransom joined us for dinner one evening, and the only sustained conversation we could handle was "How are your grandchildren?" Even worse was the night William Sloane Coffin, the activist chaplain from Yale, came for dinner. If I led the chapter in singing "Kayappa, Kayappa, Kayappa, Gayamma, I am so hayuppy tha-ut I yamma . . ." that night I have thankfully blocked it from my memory. Coffin, of course, was already condemning the escalating war in Vietnam and generally taking a few cracks at lifestyles like ours. We, who had spent the previous weekend parading around in initiation sheets and performing the solemn Victorian rituals required to initiate our pledges, were ill-equipped to defend ourselves. The chaplain so easily trapped us that we could hardly say no when he challenged us to follow him to the SDS (Students for a Democratic Society) meeting he was scheduled to address when he left our house. Slipping our pearl-encrusted Kappa keys into our pockets, we followed him with great trepidation down the alley to the University Christian Church, where the meeting was to be held. We had seen these humorless campus radicals on the steps of the Student Union. Some of us had given token support to slightly suspect University "Y" activities; others had at least signed the petition to integrate Roy's Lounge on the Drag, but we had never sat in the midst of such a group, and we shivered that our opinion on the Gulf of Tonkin might be sought. Fortunately the SDS was much too taken with Coffin even to notice us, much less explore our ignorance.

Besides the educational conflicts, the sorority could also be indicted for providing a womblike environment in which one could avoid practically all contact with the unfamiliar or unknown. Many of my sorority sisters now freely admit that they never even knew how to get to the Main Library, nor did they ever darken the door of the Chuck Wagon in the Student Union, where my roommates and I frequently drank dishwater-colored iced tea with foreign students or "rat-running" psychology lab instructors. This same narrow environment also kept the haves from developing much sensitivity for the have-nots. Sorority alumnae groups are generous philanthropists, but in college our philanthropy was usually limited to a Christmas party for blind children or an Easter egg hunt for the retarded. The only have-nots that sorority girls encountered on a regular basis were the servants in the house. I often wondered how the cook felt when the KAs rode up on horseback and sent a small black boy to the door with Old South Ball invitations on a silver tray.

Perhaps the worst indictment of the sorority system, however, is the damage done to the self-esteem of many girls by either the selection process or the values that may predominate after pledging. The same friend who recalled the gruesome pledge line insists that flowerpots dwindled after my class graduated and the standards of beauty, money, and cheerleader rah-rah became entrenched. "It was an unhappy time for me," she writes. "I wasn't like the rest and yet I didn't know what else to be. Half the time I hated myself for not being able to fill the sorority mold I had been raised to believe was what a girl should be; half the time I hated myself for even considering becoming like them. Ultimately I led a double life, holding minor service offices and doing those daring 'radical' things, like introducing motions to allow Jewish girls to go through our rush. Graduate school was my lifesaver. My experience there was so good that it tends to block out the mindlessness, the social superiority, and the hypocrisy of those undergraduate days. Looking back, I see my two years in the house as most men regard their Army duty—only mine was service to my family and their values instead of my country. It was such a waste of potential and time. My life goes so fast now, when I compare it with those hours spent on phone duty as a pledge at the sorority house."

Shortly after our graduation in 1966, a very different generation appeared, provoking many changes at the University—the Drag vendors, the use of drugs, massive demonstrations against the war, the no-bra look, the pass-fail grading system, bicycles as an acceptable mode of transportation, beer in the Student Union, the lifting of curfews in women's housing, and courses in a new discipline called Women's Studies. The whole Greek system suddenly was viewed as an anachronism surely doomed to extinction. Indeed, the Panhellenic Council removed itself in 1967 as a recognized campus organization, hence becoming no longer subject to University regulation or eligible to use University facilities. Some say this became necessary when the University discontinued supervision of student housing except that which it actually owned and operated. Sorority alums were not yet ready to abandon curfews, and they needed an independent body to govern such regulations. Others insist that sororities with racial and religious discriminatory clauses in their bylaws felt threatened. In truth, most sororities had purged their charters of such clauses long before civil rights unrest became a reality on campus. Numbers going through rush dropped drastically then; several fraternities and sororities folded, and living space in sorority houses went begging as girls moved to apartments.

The hypocrisy of the "standards committee," which served as a self-policing morals squad within most sororities, finally crumbled in many houses. In our day, the standards committee had served without much question. Headed by the sorority vice-president and assisted by an alum adviser, the committee was usually composed of girls of good character who ideally were imbued with discretion and compassion for the weaker sisters in their midst. They were charged with preserving the sorority's reputation, which occasionally involved admonishing, disciplining, or expelling those who strayed. One contemporary of mine recalled that "nymphomania" was the big scare word in standards committee. "Pledge an ugly girl, but for God's sake, don't let a nymphomaniac slip through!" The fact was, most standards committee members were intimidated by candidly rebellious behavior, and those girls who openly marched to a different moral drummer often escaped unpunished. It was the poor timid soul who, after two cups of spiked punch, vomited in the stall next to the alum chaperone at the spring formal who got called on the carpet. Apparently, when birth control pills and drugs became readily available in the late sixties, it became difficult in many houses to assemble enough straight arrows to form such a committee. Rebellion widened the gulf that already existed between sorority members and what they regarded as "interfering" alumnae. University curfews were lifted, but sorority girls were still required to be in their houses by eleven-thirty on weeknights. Repeated violations of the curfew threatened expulsion for even the officers in some of the sororities. Pappagallo shoes were being exchanged for bare feet and Army fatigues. Housemothers resigned, and alumnae wrung their hands.

So I went back to rush week in 1975. I had heard that the number of girls going through rush was rising again, but I was skeptical. I still expected to see a tired old dinosaur ready for the last rites—or a vastly revolutionized sorority system. I found neither. There I was again in the Tri Delts' front yard wiping the sweat off my upper lip. Well, a few things had changed. Panhellenic no longer lobbies for dark cottons. Dallas and Houston rushees were classy in their cool summer dresses worn fashionably three inches below the knee with rope wedges and bangle bracelets. My counterparts—girls from Edinburg and Fort Stockton—were most often represented by polyester church dresses worn three inches above the knee with pumps. Nervous conversation was unchanged. "Sounds like a mob scene in there. I'm not sure I wanta go in . . ." "I didn't even know she was an A Chi O, y'all. I hope I don't get in trouble." In the minutes before the doors burst open, there was much flopping of long hair behind ears and finally, nail biting. The yellow brick road was gone, but the gushing enthusiasm was unchanged. The rush captain, or maybe she was the president, looked like Margaux Hemingway. In fourteen years, the beauty standards had been upgraded. I wasn't permitted inside the houses—not even my own sorority house (alum pressure is out)—but from the curb I spotted the same machinery still in motion. I overheard a frantic active begging another, "Please take my second girl; I've just got to give Sally a good rush." I watched as they unself-consciously clapped, squealed, or ran out for a second goodbye hug even though a Panhellenic representative had signaled the end of the party.

In talking with active members later, I was amazed to learn how little rush really had changed. The songs, the finger snapping, and even the language were essentially the same. "She's the key to Houston" had become "She's the ticket," just as a much-admired fraternity man had gone from "stud" to "stallion." Fatigue and giddiness still prevailed in the late-night voting sessions, with a few cynical seniors sometimes tossing panties in the air and yelling, "We really rushed her pants off!" Skits are no longer the major productions they once were, but the silence rules, the maudlin sentimentality, and the weeping are still an integral part of the rush week scene. I asked about the tears. "Aren't girls just too sophisticated now for that sort of gimmickry?"

"Well," the innocents replied, "they really are a lot smarter these days and they know if you're not really sincere. But that last night, well, you just look around the room and know how glad you are to be a Kappa—well, it's just like the last night at camp, you just can't keep from crying."

"But what about the changes?" I asked. I was relieved to learn that girls receiving no bids are now called in advance by a Panhellenic representative to spare them the public humiliation of the old no-bid envelope. I was not surprised to learn that sorority pins are never worn on campus; they were beginning to fade from the scene even while I was in school. "Dressing" to go on campus has returned. I doubt seriously if the gold earrings were ever abandoned even when revolutionary garb was in fashion. Jewish girls are no longer restricted to Jewish sororities, but I saw no Spanish surnames other than those of Spanish land grant aristocracy from the Rio Grande Valley. Black sororities still exist and since 1967 have participated in Panhellenic activities and intramural sports with the white sororities.

But I also wanted to know whether the outside world had forced many changes in the sororities. "What impact has the women's movement had on sororities?" I asked.

"Not much," they shrugged. "Oh, almost everybody majors in business or communications or elementary education, but it's not because they really want careers. They just know that they've got to get a job when they graduate." I suppose I should have anticipated this response. The women's liberation movement had begun with an intellectual appeal, but most Texas women have been brought up to trust their charm more than their intellect.

"What about marriage? Do you still pass the lighted candle at chapter meetings while singing,

I found my ma-an.
He's my Kappa ma-an.
He's my sweetheart for evermore.
I'll leave him never,
I'll follow wherever he goes."

"We still pass the candle, but it hardly ever gets blown out. Not many of us are getting married after graduation, but it's not because we wouldn't like to," they giggled.

"What about no curfew?" I asked, recalling how many of my sisters had sustained injuries while sneaking out of the house. One of my contemporaries had actually broken a foot in a fall from the fire escape and had to be hauled back up through a window. She awakened the housemother with a lame story about falling down the carpeted stairway.

"Well, everybody is usually in by two a.m. and usually earlier on the weeknights," they assured me. Their parents, I learned, pay an extra $50 per semester for a security guard to let the girls in and out at night.

There was so much more that I wanted to know, but they were eager to hear about my bygone era. "Oooooh, you were here when they had Ten Most Beautiful and Bluebonnet Belles and Round Up Revue." I could tell from their curiosity that they felt cheated.

Because I sensed that I had been talking to the straight-arrow public relations team of the sorority, I deliberately sought out one of the two acknowledged scholars within the membership, a law school–bound Plan II student. Plan II (a liberal arts honors program), the college of humanities, and the college of natural sciences were poorly represented in the sorority houses I investigated. This young lady was indeed very bright, and I pressed her to justify her Greek affiliation.

"Plan II is really a tough academic program," she said, "and I study so hard during the week that if someone didn't plan some mindless social activity for me on the weekend, I'd probably crack. My friends who came here from the same private high school and didn't pledge are beginning to drop out. They just can't face four years of college without ever going to a big party."

I had called her away from an SAE street dance. She freely admitted that none of her dates on the weekend were intellectual types. "I talk about Kant and Hegel all week. I don't want any more on Saturday." She doesn't live in the house because she needs the silence of her own apartment to carry such an academic load. "I sometimes wish I'd pledged a fraternity," she grinned. "They have such a good time, dropping by their fraternity houses to shoot a game of pool, play cards, or just shoot the breeze. We only go to our sorority houses for some organized meeting—never just for the fun of it."

The Greek system died out on many campuses across the country during the late sixties. The president of UT's Interfraternity Council, noting that pledge classes and houses are full again, says, "The Greek system is definitely thriving." Of course the 5,000 people who participated in rush last year are still quite a minority on a campus of more than 40,000, even more of a minority than in the sixties when the 5,000 Greeks made up about a fifth of the campus population of 27,000. However, after several years during which rush was totally ignored by the *Daily Texan,* the irate September letters have begun to crop up again in the "Firing Line" letters column: "Only a moron would pay someone to impose rules upon them of the 'don't speak to boys during rush week' variety." "Big sisters and study buddies, indeed!" "They remind me of swine at auction." "The Greek system is composed of people with Pat Boone/Ann Landers mentality who insist on segregating themselves socially, sexually, and racially."

"I often wanted to become friends with one of those beautiful chicks with the long, flowing hair, but most of them are such conceited social climbers that I just stay away from them."

Sorority members continue to dominate certain campus activities, such as Student Union committees, simply because they are joiners and organizers by nature. The University Sweetheart is invariably a sorority girl, principally because no one else is interested and because the Greeks have the organizational power to get out the vote.

Certainly, the intimidating size of the University of Texas student body and physical plant had something to do with the returning strength of the Greek system. As one Highland Park mother put it, "When these affluent high school kids around here visit the University, they visit the sorority and fraternity people. That *is* the University to them. Not to pledge is to step into an unfathomable void." Another mother admitted that her daughter was not a particularly independent spirit. "If she's going to be a follower, we'd just as soon she be in a group where she'll at least keep up her appearance."

The nostalgia craze is certainly another factor in the sorority revival of the seventies. When I visited the campus briefly in the spring of 1976, I saw freshmen spending hours stuffing crepe paper into chicken-wire floats for the Round Up parade, a spectacular phenomenon discontinued during the sixties at UT. Sigma Chi Derby Day, with its sorority relays and "tug o' war" over mud pits, has reappeared, and Greek-sponsored dance marathons for charity have been held in Gregory Gym. Indeed, the current self-described absurdist student body president and vice-president, Jay Adkins and Skip Slyfield, make the absurdities of Greek life seem quite in tune with the times.

And perhaps it's more than just nostalgia. Some have suggested that it's a longing for tradition. You're supposed to feel something for your alma mater, aren't you? At the University of Texas, if you don't "feel it" for the Longhorns' winning tradition, the Orange Tower, and the "Eyes," you have little else to come back for. UT has no ivied halls or picturesque chapels and few legendary professors. Most students graduate by mail rather than attending the massive and impersonal graduation ceremonies. There are no formal homecomings or reunions unless you "belonged" to something while you were there—the Texas Cowboys, the Friars, the Longhorn Band, or even a sorority or fraternity, each with its own rituals and traditions.

I suppose the wisest answer to the survival question came from another sorority sister of mine. "Well, why do girls still make their debut in Dallas?" she asked. "Because people long for exclusivity, because their parents want them to, because they are only nineteen years old and are not asking the same questions that we ask at thirty-two."

I think she's right. I was recently perusing a copy of the *Kappa Key,* my sorority's national magazine, which finds me no matter where I hide. An interview with a bright-eyed blond coed caught my eye. She had been Miss Everything on her campus, and when questioned about the value of being cheerleader, homecoming queen, and sorority president, she replied, "I don't think it's always nice to question the relevance of things that are fun."

You can always wait and do that when you're thirty-two.

My Life and Hard Times in the Junior League

IN MARCH OF 1974 I was attending a Tuesday Lenten service at church when an acquaintance in the pew across the aisle caught my eye and silently mouthed, "Congratulations." I looked blankly back at her, but deep in my heart I knew what she was talking about. No woman is supposed to know that she has been proposed for membership in the Junior League, but in fact she always does. When your best friend calls asking for sixteen recent photographs of you, your Texarkana High School yearbook, the University of Texas *Cactus* for 1962 through 1966, and your mother's telephone number, what else can it mean?

The invitation to membership in the Dallas Junior League was waiting for me when I got home. Even as I read it, the telephone began to ring with more congratulations from old sorority sisters and my mother's friends. My husband even got calls at the office from other men congratulating him. But I didn't exactly share everyone else's enthusiasm. To say that I had mixed feelings about the invitation is an understatement.

On one hand I was flattered. An invitation from the Junior League is highly coveted by many Dallas women, and to decline to join would be very much like refusing a White House invitation. On the other hand, the times were out of joint for the League and me. I was in the throes of motherhood and an incipient writing career. The women's movement added to my ambivalence. I had good friends in both camps. I knew women who canceled their *Vogue* subscriptions and sometimes their marriages and women who registered for submissiveness training seminars and continued to wear Hanes hosiery because gentlemen preferred it. I straddled the fence by wearing slightly frayed blue jeans and blusher, and tried to remember which of my friends were "women" and which were "ladies." The League was clearly filled with "ladies," and in 1974 the ladies seemed anachronistic. Nevertheless, given my upbringing, I couldn't quite accept the feminist dictum that to do volunteer work is to be exploited, and if my cherished League friends cared enough to go through the machinations of getting me into this organization, how could I turn them down?

To make a long story short, I joined but I never amounted to much. Some people are born to be club women, some can be trained, and some just can't "keep a good notebook." I think I may have had my fill of *Robert's Rules of Order* in high school. I also never learned to do needlepoint, an important skill if one is to endure changes of bylaws at long organizational meetings.

Any Junior League member who passed her training course will tell you that the purpose of the Association of Junior Leagues, Inc., is "exclusively educational and charitable and is to promote voluntarism." But if that was all there was to it, we could just dispense with the reading of the minutes and go home. No, what initially fascinated me about the Junior League was that it reminded me so much of the sorority I had belonged to twelve years earlier at the University of Texas. Here we all were again with big name tags pinned to our dresses. The sorority house was now a country club or a lovely tearoom. And there were still beautiful faces, classy clothes, a selection process, songs, skits, and costumes. There were even "transfers" from less-selective Leagues—still sometimes privately referred to as "real dogs." I even perceived a glimmer of the old ideological split between the "flowerpots," those who hewed to the espoused purposes of the organization, and the "flowers," who mainly liked to get together and visit.

But, for all the similarities, the Junior League in 1979 is much more than a sorority. Because it absorbs women's energies over a longer period of time (most women remain active for at least ten years), encompasses a broader age span (from about twenty-six to forty), and performs vital volunteer services in the community, the Junior League is much harder to define. Within almost any Junior League, you will run into a little tradition, some noblesse oblige, some fierce female competition, a religious faction, a little tap dancing, and a lot of talk about dieting, dyslexia, designer dresses, and divorce. You'll also encounter huge sums of money raised for the public good, some savvy political strategists, emerging feminism, folding chairs full of balance sheets and ballots and needlepoint, and a president at the podium spouting acronyms.

During my two-year tour of duty I was what the League bureaucracy calls "a good little Indian." I worked the first year as a docent at the Museum of Natural History at Fair Park. I reasoned that knowing a little about armadillos, javelinas, raccoons, and grizzly bears would be useful to a mother of sons. I studied my docent script dutifully, memorized the slide show, and even read my older son's *Ranger Rick* magazines for bizarre animal lore.

Every Friday morning for nine months, I herded busloads of schoolchildren past the dioramas of egrets, buffaloes, and mammoth tusks. In the first corridor, the teachers seized the opportunity to desert their charges to have a smoke or hide in the bathroom. This left the docent with thirty or forty nameless children to control. Relieved to be out of their classrooms, the kids seldom exhibited much interest in my spiel. I would, for example, solicit reverence for the majestically displayed bald eagle, only to have a ten-year-old country-wise kid pop his gum and say, "Lady, you know what? My daddy calls them eagles 'blackbirds,' and they eat our baby goats like crazy. He says you can't hardly get nobody to shoot 'em no more." I would move swiftly to the rookeries of roseate spoonbills, raise hopes for a sighting of the ivory-billed woodpecker in the Big Thicket, and even work up a few tears for the brown pelican, whose eggs cracked because of the DDT in its diet.

After about six months of this, I began to hope the school buses would break down, so I could drink coffee like the paid staff and gaze in solitude at snakes in the formaldehyde jars in the basement. My League placement adviser looked aghast when I wrote down my first choice for the next year—Parkland Hospital emergency room—but I was ready for changing exhibits. Parkland, in those days, was the type of unpopular placement the League had for working women who had to get in their hours at night or on weekends. It didn't exactly attract the crowd who joined to socialize. I scoffed at a woman who said, "My husband would never let me work at Parkland."

I began at the triage desk, where all emergency patients are checked in, charted, and dispatched to special areas. The first day I registered cases of hiccups, gas, sore throat, hives—all the routine ailments of the city's indigent population. I was beginning to long for the buffaloes and mammoth tusks, when the doors burst open and the emergency paramedics rolled in the victim of a barroom stabbing. Somebody thrust a clipboard in my hand and shoved me toward the rolling cart. "Get him checked in and charted." I followed the paramedics to the surgery area, hoping that they at least knew the man's name. I tried to be cool as they stripped off the flailing man's pants and tied him with restraints to the surgical table. "Sir," I blurted timidly, "I just need to know your name for our records." He let out a string of drunken obscenities. I was ready to give up, when the paramedic slapped the patient's face and said, "Buddy, ain't nobody gonna start sewing you up till you tell that nice lady your name. Then I want you to start thinking real hard about your address and your birthday." I was afraid he might die before I got to ask him about insurance, but with the skillful paramedic's help I got all the blanks filled in and returned triumphantly to the triage desk.

Eventually I learned to take vital signs, to get patients to X-ray, to deliver lab reports, and to locate patients' charts, and my children came to regard me with the same awe they felt for the paramedics on NBC's *Emergency One*. In the course of the year, I assisted in a rape examination, helped pour charcoal down an overdosed teenager, saw a child the age of my own die before his parents could be located, met a homosexual priest in for his regular VD treatment, checked in a county jail inmate named Famous, held the hand of a thirteen-year-old in labor, changed a sanitary napkin for a woman with a broken hip, and had an extensive written conversation with a deaf man whose principal complaint seemed to be "fallen private parts."

Occasionally my bleeding heart got the best of me. When I discovered that a one-legged, diabetic black woman was planning to spend the night sitting in the hospital waiting room because the volunteer van had failed to return for her, I offered to take her home. She, of course, had never driven a car and had no sense of direction other than a vague notion of the city bus route. After two and a half hours of wandering in far South Dallas, I finally located her nursing home.

At the Crossroads

My year at Parkland was an immersion in a side of life that North Dallas matrons seldom see, but in many ways it was a textbook example of Junior League voluntarism—of the privileged helping the less privileged in a direct and personal way. Unfortunately, if the League continues on its present course, fewer members will have this experience. The reasons for this are of course complex, but the change is attributable in some part to the redefining of women's roles, to a subtle shift away from helping others to helping self, and to a loss of confidence in tradition and traditional institutions like the Junior League.

Over the past two years I have traveled to a number of Junior Leagues in Texas. I have talked with a lot of women who are confused about their roles not just as mothers, wives, and professionals but also as volunteers. Some resent that their lives have fallen into predictable patterns. Others have altered the pattern by spreading themselves dangerously thin—pursuing graduate degrees, operating businesses, selling real estate, carpooling two or three children, room-mothering, and still volunteering their almost nonexistent free hours to attend required League meetings, sing in nursing homes, save historic buildings, and sew costumes for the Junior League Ball. Some were running five miles a day and practicing transcendental meditation between eleven o'clock and midnight. I almost choked on my aspic when one of these friends said to me, "I just don't know how you find time to do all that writing."

Texas women did not need the women's movement to get them out of the house—volunteer work in the community had traditionally served that purpose. But now the feminists are telling us that volunteer work, like housework, makes women feel needed but not valued. Women who long ago decided that they were meant for better things than vacuuming the floor as housewives are also asking themselves why they should be emptying bedpans as volunteers. I'm in favor of people achieving their full potential, but if that means no one will be holding a child's hand at a free dental clinic or recording books for the blind, then the Junior League's original purpose—to organize the privileged to help the underprivileged—will be lost. And we will all be diminished because of it.

Volunteer work has been the stated purpose of the Junior League ever since a pair of nineteen-year-old New York debutantes, Mary Harriman and Nathalie Henderson, decided in 1901 to organize their leisure time for service to the community. Those founders of the Junior League were soon joined by Eleanor Roosevelt and other young women who embraced the reforming impulse of the Progressive Era. It is ironic that the Junior League, which in 1979 is widely regarded as the embodiment of tradition, was to those restless debutantes a vehicle for breaking out of their traditional sphere. Eleanor Roosevelt and her Junior League friends rejected the Four Hundred and the "season" at Newport in favor of riding streetcars or elevated trains alone into neighborhoods where male derelicts staggered out of saloons. Working in the settlement houses of the Lower East Side, these women saw misery and exploitation on a level they had never imagined.

Junior Leagues have existed in Texas for about fifty years, and they are thriving today. Like the New York League, the Texas organization drew its initial membership from clearly defined ranks of society. In the twenties, of course, upper-class women were the only ones with enough leisure time to organize. "How we adored the Junior League then!" said Mrs. James Nixon, a Philadelphia-born founder of the San Antonio Junior League, in an interview with Susan Hamilton of the *San Antonio Light*. "We held meetings every day. They used to tease that I'd go to the Children's Free Clinic to work while my own babies were sick at home with the maid. It was true. But it was so easy to get good help then." Apart from these Lady Bountiful activities, League members frequently spent their time hostessing innumerable fund-raising teas and luncheons. Such tearoom socializing made the Leagues appear frivolous, but in fact the proceeds from such lunchrooms helped to finance another type of lunchroom—the Salvation Army soup kitchens, which by 1931 were feeding the millions of Americans caught in the Depression.

In the early forties the Junior Leagues were predictably involved in the war effort. By the fifties, Junior League thrift shops flourished, as did garden clubs, style-show benefits, canasta luncheons, and rummage sales. No one questioned whether reading stories at Scottish Rite Crippled Children's Hospital or staffing a mobile X-ray unit would prepare a woman for a midlife career. If a woman wanted to dress up like Cinderella for ten years in the children's theater performances, no one worried that she might be stifling her "growth potential."

The fifties and early sixties were the halcyon days of Junior Leagues. Volunteer work was what every woman did if her husband was a good provider. League activities were regularly reported on the front page of the newspaper society section through the early sixties. "The League lost a big motivating force," one older member laments, "when the Women's Section of the paper changed to Trend." Newspaper coverage, of course, is not the only thing that has changed. Texas' cities have grown at unprecedented rates, so defining the boundaries of "society" has become extremely complicated. And inflation has meant that charitable donations, unless linked with federal grants or matching funds, cannot accomplish what they once did.

Perhaps the most significant changes have occurred in the lives of upper-middle-class women themselves. They go to school longer. Ten percent of the Dallas Junior League members have graduate degrees. League women now marry later than they did a decade ago, and they sometimes postpone childbirth until their thirties. They have less household help than their mothers did.

Life for the Junior League woman is often as hectic and strained as it is for a full-time working mother, but the League member has the added pressure of maintaining the appearance of a stay-at-home wife and mother—and little reward when someone at a cocktail party asks the inevitable "What do you do?" Women with preschool children frequently find themselves serving on committees and competing with older women whose children are in school five days a week. Making expensive day care arrangements to do volunteer work doesn't make economic sense; consequently, children often get stashed with a friend's maid or dropped at a variety of church day care centers in the course of a week. Small wonder that the children of one League member applauded wildly when they saw what they took to be a For Sale sign on the headquarters of the Houston Junior League.

Many people agree that the Junior League should make forty the minimum age for admission rather than the maximum age for active membership. However, the League has always maintained that if the habit of volunteering is not instilled in women at an early age, they seldom find time for it later. As it stands, though, a lot of League women are so burned out at forty that they never employ their valuable training again. Some of the Leagues in Texas have recently raised their maximum admission age to thirty-six, but I suspect it was a move to temporarily swell the dwindling ranks of those members between the ages of thirty-four and forty, who do the bulk of the League's work. Younger women admitted to the League are often professionals who have no ambition to make the League their full-time career.

Another influence on even the most conservative upper-middle-class women, of course, is the women's movement. Older women who had volunteered years of their lives to community service were dismayed to hear their career-bound daughters say, "Gee, Mom, I'll bet you're sorry you wasted all that time doing volunteer work." But what really jolted the Junior League was the defection of some of its most promising members to careers. One early defector said to me, "The Junior League? It seems like that happened in another life. I can hardly remember it at all." Now, with the first wave of the women's movement past, fewer young professional women defect. Leagues hold separate night meetings for working women. Nearly 30 percent of the Dallas and Houston League members are gainfully employed. This organization that once was characterized as "We don't do, we are" is now being asked by its younger members, "What do you do that is worth my time?"

The Junior League is under pressure from its members to provide "meaningful placement." By "meaningful" most women mean something they can use on a résumé sheet for a "real job." With divorce on the rise, even the most traditional women are assessing their marketable skills. No matter how much praise President Carter, Erma Bombeck, and Lynda Johnson Robb heap on motherhood and volunteer work, many contemporary women still fumble when filling in the "occupation" blank on the supermarket check-cashing card. If being a volunteer is the appropriate and fulfilling role for affluent women, then why are Charlotte Ford and Gloria Vanderbilt autographing the back pockets of blue jeans?

The national Junior League organization got the message and designed a program called Volunteer Career Development. Sensitive to the feelings of older members who might be threatened by the word "career," the Dallas League mulled the program over for a year or so, then renamed it Focus. A gentle consciousness-raising group, Focus encourages women to consider their interests and talents and choose volunteer placements that will increase skills in those areas. "There is no pressure to select a paid career as the ultimate goal," said a League member who has taught the course, "but we do want women to take responsibility for their lives and to realize that they have already made certain choices whether they were aware of them or not."

What League activities are transferable to a résumé? Raising and disbursing large sums of money, all with increased scrutiny from the IRS, are bound to credit at least a few members with some financial expertise. There is also experience to be gained in compiling and marketing cookbooks and other pamphlets, selling advertising, writing press releases, and applying for grants. And as the League becomes more involved in publicly funded projects, members who deal with elected officials are becoming very sophisticated politically.

Unfortunately the majority of these "meaningful" jobs are found in the bureaucracy of the Junior League, which doesn't bode well for an organization that is supposed to train community volunteers. The more status and prestige the League attaches to organizational work, the more the League will produce organizational women who do little good for anyone other than themselves and the League. This dilemma greatly concerns certain League women. One member captured it in a recent editorial in the Dallas League's magazine: "If the League can't build up some old-time enthusiasm for volunteering, we may find that we are just shifting around deck-chair assignments on the *Titanic.*"

The League was founded on the principle that a woman's two primary responsibilities are to her family and her community, but the Dallas League estimates that by next year half its members will be professionals. No matter how you stretch it, it's hard to make the old-time volunteer spirit fit in with a full-time job. For example, a working woman gives only thirty-five hours a year to her League volunteer work, and by necessity she has to pursue it at night or on weekends. No doubt the League, which still employs male lawyers and accountants, could draw on its professional members to perform those skills, but how does that help the community?

Just why a woman with a full-time career wants to be in the League in the first place puzzles me a little. I cannot rule out a genuine desire to perform altruistic service, although I seldom heard that motivation mentioned by the working women I interviewed. One young lawyer admitted she was in the League for her mother. "You know how mothers are. I attended a great undergraduate school, graduated with honors, went to law school, graduated in the top five percent, and was hired by a prestigious law firm. So what does my mother say? 'Oh, honey, you never were in a sorority. The Junior League is your last chance.'" Another young professional admitted that the man she intended to marry was likely to be transferred and she thought the League would be a good contact to have in any community. Others said that their jobs were socially confining and they valued the opportunities the League offers to be with friends. But when professionals dominate the Junior League, will it become just another civic club, like the Lions, Kiwanis, or Rotary?

Why We Join

In spite of its identity crisis, the League still attracts women who simply want to help others. Those of us raised in the Bible Belt on "Freely ye have received, freely give" grew up with the expectation of helping other people. While Woody Allen and his playmates were seeing their analysts, my hometown friends and I were holding vacation Bible school in the tar-paper shacks of a gypsy camp on the outskirts of town. We spent some summers sprawled in the sun beside swimming pools, but we also scrubbed lousy heads and aired urine-soaked mattresses at the Community Chest camp for underprivileged children. Women don't join the Junior League just so they can help the handicapped, but many of them grew up doing volunteer work and planned to continue as adults. The immediate past president of the Dallas Junior League was a candy striper at Baylor Hospital when she was fourteen.

In an organization like the Dallas League, however, with more than a thousand upper-middle-class women, motivations are bound to vary. To be sure, many women have never given their membership a second thought. The Junior League is as inevitable as living in Highland Park or joining the country club. Some, however, have a genuine sense of noblesse oblige. These are the members who probably never needed the League to give them the stamp of social approval in the first place. They are well-educated women who do not seem to suffer guilt about leaving their children and their kitchen largely in the care of servants. They assume volunteer responsibilities as full-time careers, and they usually rise quickly in the power structure. They are seldom found handling snakes at the zoo or gluing Popsicle sticks with a Mexican American child at the Inner City Day Camp.

Instead, they appear on the boards of United Way or Mental Health and Mental Retardation, or perhaps on the board of the Museum of Fine Arts, the symphony, or the opera. Articulate and almost intimidating advocates for their favorite causes, these women can usually muster League funds and volunteers to keep projects afloat.

Other women admit that they need the Junior League to give them self-confidence in dealing with the community. These women may have the same intelligence and perhaps more money than those of the noblesse, but they lack the power and the connections. Being a member of the Junior League enables a woman to go to the top of any agency or institution for information or funding. As one member said, "When something goes awry in the school system, the Junior League member can call the superintendent and not be shuffled off by his secretary to a double-talking member of the bureaucracy."

Several Texas Junior Leagues recently surveyed their members, using a questionnaire created by the Hogg Foundation. It revealed that most women valued above all else the "sociability" that the Junior League provided them. "Sociability" was described as "working with congenial, interesting women, doing interesting things that enable me to escape the routines of housework, and the opportunity to develop friendships." Although these may not be the motives envisioned by the idealistic founders of the Junior League, who can fault an organization for providing "sociability" in an age when women are isolated in the suburbs or move often from city to city?

No one appreciates her League membership more than a woman whose corporate-executive husband is frequently transferred. The Houston and Dallas Junior Leagues, for example, are hard-pressed to keep native-born members in the majority. The immediate past president of the Houston League is a transfer from Tyler. In Dallas each transfer is assigned a "friend" who goes with her to meetings and provides her with the emotional support and information that next-door neighbors used to offer.

Of course, you don't have to be a transfer to reap the serendipitous benefits offered by League membership. There is probably no better place to hear about the best schools, the preferred teacher, or an orthodontist within bike-riding distance. The Junior League is a perpetual source of information about decorators, seamstresses, hairdressers, Colorado condominiums, summer camps, exercise classes, maids, caterers, house painters, carpenters, divorce lawyers, and plastic surgeons. League members with realtor's licenses also know that it is an invaluable source of rumors about prime real estate.

For some women the Junior League fills a void left by ambitious husbands. "Jogging is about the only thing my husband and I do together anymore," one League member in her mid-thirties told me, "and you don't get a lot of meaningful conversation out of your husband when you're huffing around a track at six in the morning." I've asked some League members' husbands what they thought of their wives' involvement in the League, and one only half-facetiously replied, "Well, it keeps her off the bottle and out of the shopping malls. I think it's great!" "He wants me to have something to do so he won't feel guilty about never being home," says a busy League officer. "You know how it is being married to a lawyer."

"It's my one contact with the outside world," one woman said of her Junior League involvement. She was not being ironic. For women who went from the arms of their generous Texas daddies to the arms of ambitious and protective husbands and then settled comfortably into the same neighborhoods and country clubs where they had grown up, the Junior League can be a liberating force. One League member in a small town told me that her association with the Junior League had sent her to conferences in Boston, San Francisco, and Washington, D.C. "I had never traveled anywhere without my husband. Because of the Junior League, I was thrown on my own resources—handling baggage, hailing cabs, tipping, checking into hotels. These may seem like small things to some women, but it was a real accomplishment and self-confidence booster for me."

Anyone who joins the Junior League with the expectation of improving her social life is likely to be disappointed. Perhaps in the past, when the Dallas League was smaller, becoming a member automatically placed one in a social circle. Today, however, when monthly meetings gather six or seven hundred women, it is difficult to feel any cozy exclusivity. "The Junior League isn't as much fun as it used to be," one sustaining member ("sustainer" being the lovely League euphemism for inactive members over forty) lamented. "Everything is so busy and too serious. If anybody has a party, it has to have a purpose—stamping out cancer or saving the symphony." Those who believe the Highland Park Junior Leaguer meets her lunch bunch at the S&S Tea Room in Highland Park Village every day are dead wrong. The majority of the members either eat no lunch (League women are notoriously slim) or lap yogurt at stoplights on their way to pick up their carpoolers before going on to another meeting, seminar, or book club. Businessmen, it turns out, are not the only upholders of the Dallas work ethic.

The Chosen Few

What assures the League's prestige and strength and what sets the Junior Leagues in Texas apart from other women's volunteer organizations is that one does not volunteer to join. Bylaws vary slightly from League to League (there are eighteen Junior Leagues in Texas), but in Dallas a candidate must meet certain residency requirements and be between the ages of twenty-three and thirty-five. One member must propose her, and two must second. The general membership then takes a straw vote, which helps the Admissions Committee make the final decision. So how does a woman get proposed? Surprisingly, a high profile of volunteer accomplishments in the community won't always open the door. Like Episcopal salvation, membership is the gift conferred on women in certain neighborhoods, not as a reward for their good works but because they are believed to have the "potential" for good works. Every year about two hundred Dallas women are proposed for the Junior League. About ninety are selected.

Being a daughter of a League member is no longer an assurance of a place in the League, but it certainly enhances the possibility. In some cases it seems to be easier for an "outsider" to get in, provided she has married well and is rumored to be well connected elsewhere. "No one will know whom her mother has offended if she's from out of town," said one member. Texas Leagues, in which many members matriculated no further away than a Texas university, are especially enamored of women who graduated from Wellesley, Vassar, or Smith. But plenty of women become Junior Leaguers just because their friends are. Because membership depends a good deal on being known by a substantial share of people in the League, it helps to have crossed paths with them perhaps at Camp Waldemar, as a Theta at UT, or at least as a cafeteria volunteer at the Highland Park schools. "I'm sure there really are cute girls in East Dallas and elsewhere who didn't go to Highland Park High School or Hockaday or SMU who would make marvelous League members," said one well-meaning if somewhat protected young Dallas matron, "but where would we ever meet them?"

This admissions procedure is what gives the Junior League its social cachet, as well as its image problems. To outsiders the setup may recall the cruel games we played as little girls—forming secret clubs, whimsically voting each other "in" or "out." Others are quick to dismiss it as an extension of sorority life. Indeed, until recently women who were not known by the Admissions Committee in Dallas were invited to tea parties or luncheons very much like rush parties, except that the "rushee" supposedly had no idea she was being scrutinized.

Is it like sorority rush? Does anybody at age thirty stand up and say, "But yew-all, her hair is so tacky"? Most of the women I know who have served as Admissions Committee members regard their job as a burden, but they describe the selection process as more mature and fair than college sorority cutting sessions. "We're looking for intelligent, responsible women who are willing to work. Sure, we consider where she came from and who her mother is, but that's because we think a girl is likely to be a better volunteer if she grew up in a family where community service was valued." I gathered that beauty queens get closer scrutiny than they did in college. Indeed, one member suggested, "This just may be where the pots get revenge over the flowers." Opinions of members who have worked with a candidate on a PTA board apparently carry far more weight than a catty remark like "had round heels in high school."

Who doesn't get in? The League has made some concessions—a handful of Jews here, a member with a Spanish surname there, and perhaps a few black transfers—but it remains almost exclusively a WASP enclave. Also, women who have independently distinguished themselves in some area of community service may be passed over as "not needing the League." After all, the League's stated purpose is to train volunteers, not reward them. In this respect the League is full of catch-22s. I have heard friends remark, "I'm so glad Ann got in the League. She really needed it." This is an interesting bit of in-house charity that Junior Leagues provide. Women with physical beauty, apparent poise, and marriages to successful men can still be remarkably lacking in self-esteem and confidence. Some are still measuring themselves by poor academic performances years ago in college. Others just flounder without much purpose from exercise class to bridge club to tennis lesson to shopping center. The League can make a remarkable difference for these women. Getting in requires no affirmative action on their part. Being chosen is an ego boost, and some of them go on to discover useful talents they had never thought to value.

If the whole idea of being voted into a club at age thirty seems ridiculous, one must remember that most of these women have been in training for these hurdles since the second grade. And their daughters are in training now. One exasperated mother said to me, "Dammit, Prudence, if you had daughters, you couldn't even write this article. Don't you realize that most of us stay active in sorority alum groups and do our League work because we want our daughters to have those options?" The mothers of daughters are right. I don't understand. But if it's true—if all of this way-paving and place-holding does go on—I can only congratulate the Junior League for harnessing the energies of socially ambitious mothers into purposeful activity. As one sustaining member wryly commented, "Why, the Junior League does more good than the First Baptist Church. One thousand women in Dallas and almost that many in Houston who could be playing tennis are spending at least a half day a week doing something in the community's interest."

Why? Because the Junior League in Texas is ruthless in its discipline. Either a member fulfills her commitment for ninety hours of volunteer work each year (thirty-five for professional members) or she is figuratively put in the stocks. In Dallas, a suspended member is virtually ostracized from League activity and has her name published—the ignominy!—in the *News Sheet.* Every year the League yearbook prints the names of those who have paid their fines, mended their ways, and returned to the fold. Also included in the yearbook are the names of the unrepentant expulsions. They are listed just before the In Memoriams.

The Good It Does

In many parts of the Dallas community, the League is thought to be elitist, privileged, and frivolous. Meeting in country clubs, offering prayers for heavenly blessings on what has to be one of the most blessed gatherings in Dallas, and touring the county jails or juvenile detention centers attired in silk blouses and gold earrings perpetuate the image of slightly wacky Lady Bountifuls. Every new League member must complete what is called a provisional course, which takes her through public facilities, municipal agencies, and blighted neighborhoods, but even with that exposure many women remain remarkably insulated from the rest of the world. Not long ago a group of League provisionals toured Parkland Hospital's maternity facilities for charity patients (many of them unwed mothers) with a staff obstetrician. When the tour was over, the physician agreed to answer questions. One young matron raised her hand and asked, "Are the parents given Lamaze childbirth classes so the fathers can be present in the delivery room?"

One of the men who called to congratulate my husband when I got in the Junior League is a judge who, when we see him at some social gathering, never fails to say, "Here's that cute little wife of yours. I bet she's just keeping herself so busy with that Junior League that you have to cook your own supper." Though I always cringe at his remarks, there are certainly aspects of the Junior League that elicit a patronizing tone from men. Things that go on in women's circles have always seemed a little ridiculous to men. To check roll (Dallas members must attend at least three monthly meetings per year) women remove huge decorated name tags, usually hot pink, from a tag board and wear them when they enter a meeting. Names left on the board, of course, are recorded as absent. I never attended a League meeting without someone either making an announcement in doggerel, wearing a costume, performing a corny skit, or thanking her committee ad nauseam—and sometimes all four happened in one meeting. In 1974, my own provisional class stood and sang a tribute to our leaders to the tune of "Jeremiah Was a Bullfrog."

I am assured by good friends who have remained active that much of the silliness and some of the naiveté are gone from the Junior League. It's mostly big business now. The meetings are rife with business school acronyms—MBO (Management by Objectives), VCD (Volunteer Career Development), and AMP (Association Management Process). And the League's new forte is not voluntarism but fund-raising.

The Dallas Junior League Ball last year topped all Dallas charity balls by raising $350,000. The Junior League Ball, a story in itself, now absorbs the talents and energies of some Dallas League members for nine months out of the year. Choosing a woman to head the ball committee is almost more important than choosing a League president, since she must have sufficient charisma to attract a coterie of other women willing to give overtime service. Their efforts culminate in an almost flawless two-night performance at the Fairmont Hotel in January.

The show is written gratis by Dallas attorney Doug Perry, who usually adapts his own lyrics to current Broadway show tunes, and Shakespeare Festival producer Bob Glenn is the director. Competition for parts in the show is fierce. Some women and their husbands take tap dancing lessons before the auditions. The more than 2,500 people who attended the ball last year were greeted by "walking ads"—selected League members dressed like Carmen Miranda, with huge flower-and-fruit headdresses and leggy, strapless sequined costumes. Support hose do wonders for ripply thighs, but it's a dedicated Leaguer indeed who will don such a costume and wear a placard that reads, NEUHOFF BROTHERS PACKERS.

"Special ladies," representing Dallas businesses that donated greater sums of money, swooped gracefully across the stage in dazzling gowns and assumed exaggerated poses while an announcer called out the donor company's name as it flashed on a screen. Sometimes the sophisticated presentation was undercut by the prosaic name of the company—Vent-A-Hood, for example.

The show itself is remarkably professional. Several members who appear year after year undoubtedly could have had stage careers. A lot of frustrated acting talent is released on those two nights. "It's a very physical evening," said one League member. "The year I worked backstage we had a heck of a time getting the walking ads out of their pushup bras and fishnet hose and into their more sedate ball gowns. I think they rather enjoyed all of the attention they were getting, and because it was done in the name of charity, nobody could raise an eyebrow."

Motivations for participation in the show vary, but there is no doubt that it is a chance for attractive women to display themselves to an appreciative audience. During the "special lady" presentation I heard a man say to my husband, "Do you ever get to New York? Well, I'll tell you, it's just awesome how lousy the New York women look. Now look up there at that gorgeous little thing. You'd never guess that she's thirty-nine and has five kids."

The League can raise money, but it sometimes runs into problems in administering the funds. Part of the trouble stems from the simple social conditioning of upper-middle-class women, which is both a curse and a blessing for members. Women who are conditioned never to ask embarrassing questions find it difficult to hold directors of community projects accountable for sums of money the League has granted. "We have to get over this idea that the League's goal in life is to have people love us," said one member. "There is an inherent danger in becoming a successful fund-raising organization. The group develops the attitude that if we take so much money from the community, we can't offend anyone in the way we use it."

Conditioning may work against those women within the League as well. "Who ever heard of men asking permission to disagree?" said one disgruntled member. "We waste a lot of time placating each other in the internal structure. League board meetings are sometimes places where we just compliment each other on 'nice' reports rather than square off and debate the issues. Unfortunately, we sometimes save the real controversy for the kitchen telephone gossip later in the day. We still haven't learned to depersonalize our projects."

On the other hand, some of that conditioning can be a plus. League women are usually socially adept and often very manipulative. Recently, some Dallas League members employed their political know-how in support of Letot Academy, a facility for juvenile delinquents funded by the county, the Junior League, and the Dallas Independent School District. Figuring that juvenile justice programs never have sustained priority with politicians since children don't vote or pay taxes, the Leaguers arranged a ceremony celebrating the first anniversary of the academy. The word went out among the League women involved: "Wear a business suit, a cotton shirt, no jewelry, and don't let our president quote Aristotle. Let the politicians take full credit for all of your work. Invite First Lady Rita Clements, a former Dallas Junior League president, to speak and pose with elected officials for pictures documenting how successful the project is." At the end of the ceremony, a knowing district court judge rose and said, "Gentlemen, the successful launching of this project is directly attributable to these coldly calculating young women." There was a day when the League would have considered such praise an insult.

"We've learned to be very cautious about the image we project," explained one very capable advocate. "Three Junior League women dressed to the nines can turn what should be a serious negotiation into a tea party. We try to avoid those situations where someone says in a patronizing tone, 'Gentlemen, we are so pleased to have these nice ladies from the Junior League with us today.' There is less of that condescension now that we've learned to listen more and speak only when we've done our homework."

After sitting in on meetings with county commissioners, school board officials, or city council members, these League members are often amazed to discover how much influence they wield as representatives of the Junior

League. The League has steadfastly refused ever to rattle a political or economic saber, but elected officials are aware of the potential political and economic power of two thousand North Dallas taxpayers.

The League traditionally supports a broad spectrum of laudable child-related projects. The Dallas League has, for example, earmarked $300,000 for a children's wing on the city's proposed new art museum. Only this year, however, did the Dallas League address the issue of battered women. The League will pay the salary of a director for a shelter operated by the Domestic Violence Intervention Alliance. "There is still a feeling among some members," said one impatient League woman, "that nice ladies just don't talk about domestic violence or teenage pregnancy, even though both probably occur within our own ranks."

Not all Junior League members are squeamish or sheltered. Those who volunteer, for example, at juvenile detention centers or who counsel pregnant teenagers are shorn of useless idealism rather quickly. "Most of us come to projects like these believing that all these kids need is a good dose of middle-class values," admitted one Letot Academy volunteer. "We come armed with *Grimm's Fairy Tales* and *Huckleberry Finn* and plans for trips to the symphony. Within a few weeks we're elated if someone wants to read a comic book. We also learn to respect their skill at coping. They wouldn't survive a minute in their neighborhoods with the golden rule." With drastically revised expectations, some of these women become involved in "child advocacy," a current catch phrase in League circles. "We're not so idealistic as to believe that institutions will change the circumstances of these children's lives, but at least we can see that the institutions themselves do no further harm," said one woman involved in a program for truants, runaways, and other young offenders.

Women who are face to face with community problems and who are actively engineering public policy are not in the majority in the League. And their opinions do not necessarily reflect mainstream League attitudes. Nevertheless, those women are essential to the League's image of itself. League members who personally have no desire to be on the cutting edge of public policy mentioned these women to me time and time again. Indeed, there seems to be a dichotomy in "who we wish we were" and "who we are willing to be." In the Hogg Foundation's survey, the Dallas League members considered criminal justice as the area of greatest need in their community. They then ranked it sixth as appropriate for League action. It slid to ninth place on the chart that showed members' "willingness to work in the area." Cultural enrichment, on the other hand, was not considered an area of great need in the community, but it topped all others—child welfare, public education, health and welfare services, and drug abuse—in willingness to work.

Figures like these are easily manipulated. They may be interpreted as evidence of great hypocrisy or they may be seen as the League members' honest assessment of their capabilities. Most League members are undoubtedly better equipped to give art museum tours than to give birth control advice to a minority teenager. And although working with minorities ranked lowest in league members' preferences, the survey still showed that 43 percent of the women were willing to work in that area.

Junior League women are easy targets for cynical stereotyping. One League member used to say facetiously, "You can always tell a Junior League woman. She has short frosted blond hair, drives a station wagon, does needlepoint, wears espadrilles, attends at least one exercise class, has at least one child with dyslexia, has just had an affair with the tennis pro or a recent religious conversion, and still identifies her women friends by their sorority affiliations." Unfortunately, even facetious stereotypes get in the way when we try to assess the contributions of organizations. Regardless of their motivation, League members work hard at the jobs they are assigned, and they bring to these jobs a kind of middle-class dedication and attention to detail that are increasingly scarce even in paid occupations. Their efforts may not bring about great social change, but by providing volunteers and funds for museums, zoos, libraries, hospitals, juvenile detention centers, and inner-city day camps, they continue to maintain and enhance the quality of life in our towns and cities at a time when most baby boomers are content to spend their leisure hours reading *How to Flatten Your Stomach.*

A Good Little Indian Bids Her Farewell

My stint at the Parkland Hospital emergency room wasn't what prompted my resignation from the Junior League. My problem was that I never was organized enough to be a club woman. My baby-sitter supply was never adequate, and quite frankly I often preferred the company of my small boys to an inspirational League speaker. A third pregnancy caused me to write a resignation letter that went something like this:

Ladies:

While I admire greatly the capable, efficient women of the Junior League of Dallas, alas, I am not one. Unlike Dr. Seuss's Cat in the Hat, I cannot hold up the cup and the milk and the cake, the books, toy man, and the fish on a rake. I guess what I'm trying to say is: I do not own a crock pot, make casseroles in advance, or even remember to thaw the meat until five o'clock. I forget about tulip bulbs in the refrigerator, and my house will never do for a group meeting. My geraniums bloom only once. Although I trust it won't reflect on my sponsors, I must confess that I am the sort of woman who makes her whole family late to church because she has to get panty hose at the Seven-Eleven. With a new baby and a book contract, the situation can only get worse. Please accept my resignation while I am still in good standing.

In the best of League tradition, the corresponding secretary called to say that my resignation letter had been read aloud at the board meeting, and seldom had a resignation been so enjoyed. And if I didn't object, they would like to use the Cat in the Hat portion as a tribute to the outgoing president. "We might needlepoint it on a pillow for her," the secretary said.

See what I mean about efficient, capable League women? Nothing is wasted. If you have nothing else to offer, they'll needlepoint your resignation.

Reconcilable Differences

FOUR MALES share this house with me. They range in age from fourteen to forty-seven. I'm in love with all of them. They make me laugh. They make me think. They also make me cry. The occasional and shocking isolation I feel in their midst has propelled me to my typewriter for more than a decade to sort out the truth.

Men are not like women. Lately scientific research, best-selling books, and countless newspaper stories are cautiously confirming what I've observed for twenty years in this house with my husband and three sons. After decades of denying or downplaying gender differences, it is suddenly okay to speculate that certain traits are inherent. This acknowledgment of differences doesn't mean that men and women are doomed to incompatibility. To the contrary, an understanding of the different lenses through which males and females perceive the world may promote harmony. In a long and satisfactory marriage, I can also attest, some sharing of the bifocals inevitably occurs.

We are not always so different. And we are never more eager to emphasize our alikeness than when we first fall in love.

John was the teaching assistant in a history course I was taking, so I set my alarm early and feigned interest in his eight o'clock section as well. I was an English major. He took me to see Richard Burton's *Hamlet* on our first date, and later created a corny but endearing scavenger hunt for me with clues full of literary allusions. He took me to the opera in San Antonio and to the ballet in Dallas. We played chess in Austin's Eastwood Park. He delivered a convincing toast in Spanish at a party. He brought me books I didn't understand, a ploy he now admits he appropriated from the Danish philosopher Kierkegaard. Grossly oversimplified, the philosophy was: Make her think you are only interested in her mind.

When we married, there seemed to be no interest that we did not share. Evidence of our differences showed up early in the honeymoon, that extended period of too much togetherness that enables the beloveds to shed whatever illusions the courtship may have created. He was no longer exclusively interested in my mind. We traveled as students for two and a half months in Europe, time enough for him to grow to loathe my suitcase full of shoes and my penchant for eating all of the croissants in the basket in the train station, and time enough for me to wonder if I could live with a man who would forgo the Ghiberti doors in Florence to finish reading an Ian Fleming thriller in the *pensione.* On the trains I beat him like a drum at gin rummy and he sulked. My French failed us in Paris; his Spanish, in Barcelona. We had no place to run. It was the beginning of wisdom. We stopped playing card games. I took day trips on my own to see Renaissance treasures while he smoked Cuban cigars, sampled European beers, and poked through old book stalls in search of another James Bond. I came to dinner with tales of demonstrative Italians I'd met and a head count of the martyrdoms of Saint Sebastian that he'd missed. He gave me an update from the *International Herald Tribune* and the location of a trattoria where he'd sampled a local delicacy. We are still married.

Our differences persist. A pair of framed snapshots amid family pictures on the wall show him looking his happiest proudly displaying a rainbow trout in Montana; my own goofy grin is captured fresh from the reading room at the British Museum in a London tea shop. He is a lawyer and appropriately obsessive-compulsive. He loves to make lists. He leaves the house at 8:15 already focused on a day divided on a desk calendar into billable hours. Briefcase in hand, he pauses to kiss me at the door and says, as if dictating a memo, "If you have time today, could you do as follows: (a) get my blue pants at the cleaners, (b) call about tennis lessons for the kids, (c) straighten out that MasterCard error." I laugh and reply in my best legalese, "Moreover, by copy of this letter all other counsel of record will be provided a copy of the above. In addition, please add section (d) measure out life in coffee spoons."

I am a writer and a mother. Neither job lends itself to the precision that he envisions for his day. Much of my writing material comes from the ironies I run across quite by accident.

My husband is publicly a very private person. Waiters who introduce themselves irritate him. By contrast, I establish instant rapport with strangers in elevators between floors at the public library. What began as a day of writing for me in the humanities section of the library can become a day of checking downtown shelters for a homeless woman and her two babies whom I encountered in the ladies' room. From a female perspective, the male way of engaging seems unnecessarily unpleasant, lonely, and frankly, a little primitive. It often precludes the serendipitous exchanges of wit and warmth that I experience with friends and strangers daily.

"Sidetracked again?" John says incredulously as I review my unexpectedly intriguing day at dinner.

Early in our marriage, I worried that my husband seemed constitutionally unable to "pass the time of day." Social small talk does not come easy for him even now. I can still see him sitting glumly in a room with some of my mother's women friends. One turned to him in the midst of the chatter and said in a polite attempt to include him, "And what do you think about that, John?" "Frankly, Mrs. McClure," he said, "I haven't heard a word that's been said." In the remarkable way Southern women have of embroidering around such bluntness, she said, "Oh, Prudence, I can see why you married this man. Isn't his candor charming?"

Sometimes. Yes. If both of us were constantly bent on connection, life could become exhausting. Women sometimes suffer from an overabundance of rapport. My husband yawns and announces that he's going to bed if our guests have not made a move to leave on their own by midnight. I used to marvel at his ability to get our sons in bed in fifteen seconds flat, a particularly welcome skill when they were preschoolers. When I was in charge, the tuck-me-in chore always consumed most of the evening, since I was determined that no one go to bed angry or unforgiven. In most cases, I was the only one who remembered the day's slights or transgressions.

"Do the necessary," he says to our boys. The male ability to solve problems is surely part of what attracts us. When a cat left a baby squirrel only half dead on our front porch last week, my husband, already dressed for work, matter-of-factly picked up a hammer and bonked the squirrel out of its misery. I would have searched for a shoe box, called an animal rescue center, and generally done a lot of hand-wringing involving many more people before arriving at such a sensible solution.

Of course, it is the reluctance to look beyond "the necessary" that often gets men in trouble. Sometimes even our views of doing the necessary are different. On returning tired from a family trip, I surveyed the refrigerator and determined that a trip to the grocery store was required before we could have dinner. My husband opened the freezer and said, "Well, I could just eat this chicken potpie." "Great," I snapped, "I'm glad you got *yourself* taken care of." He was genuinely surprised at the venom in my tone. He thought he was doing me some sort of favor by assuming responsibility for his own meal. As one who regularly prepares meals for five, I never think of the meal as the sum of its parts. One less mouth to feed didn't obviate the need for the grocery run. To this day, when someone stands aimlessly in front of the open refrigerator, my husband cautions, "Don't reach for that chicken potpie."

My husband says that most men feel bad about their misreading or failure to understand their wives' messages. "I was so relieved when she took up tennis," one of his friends told him. "She quit coming at me with that yellow tablet to write down goals for our lives. She thinks because I don't talk about the things that bother me that I don't think about them either."

In an article in the *Washington Post,* columnist Richard Cohen wrote, "I wonder if something inherent in men makes them less communicative than women, less able to say how they feel. . . . They are like some primitive fish, looking from the sea to the land, wanting to take that next evolutionary step, but lacking little legs." A woman friend of mine says her husband only discusses problems after he's solved them. Most men do not or cannot avail themselves of the therapy that women provide each other daily by trading fears, anxieties, and failures.

Nothing separates us more than tears. Rosie Grier can sing "It's All Right to Cry" till the cows come home and the men in my life won't believe it. My husband refuses to see movies or read books involving fatal illnesses, nuns, sick or handicapped children, or doomed animals. After *Field of Dreams,* I suppose he'll be more cautious about baseball movies. One of my sons watched *West Side Story* with me when he was seven. In the final sad scene, he wiped the tears from his eyes, jumped up, and said with a look of total betrayal, "Thanks for not telling me it was going to end like that!" I explain to them that my own tears, a weapon of last resort when all understanding has broken down, are really a wonderful tension release. "They may release your tension," they say, "but they sure increase ours."

They fear my tears and worry when I don't return at an appointed hour that I have carried out the trash (which I had hoped they'd do without being told) and kept on going down the alley, leaving them forever. After nearly twenty-five years of marriage, my husband muses that I am still here only because of my marvelous power of imagination. He says that I must believe that when we are unburdened by children and the pressures of court deadlines, the old romantic will emerge once again to quote a Shakespearean sonnet, perhaps surprise me with an elegant toast in Spanish, or at least lecture me on the rise of the right wing in American politics as he once did after too much champagne at a wedding reception the night we met. A character in British author Barbara Pym's novel *Jane and Prudence* put it this way:

> *But of course, she remembered, that was why women were so wonderful, it was their love and imagination that transformed these unremarkable beings . . . perhaps love affairs with handsome men tended to be less stable because so much less sympathy and imagination were needed on the women's part.*

I'm not going anywhere. We are who we are. And he is no slacker when it comes to imagination. Despite my gray-streaked hair, early-morning sinus trouble, and egg-stained robe, he still thinks I am a college beauty queen and that he's lucky to have a date with me for the weekend. He regularly says as much in front of his sons. All of their lives, my sons have lived with two people who have great respect for one another, who willingly share the thankless, boring tasks of life, who have never perceived their life together as a power struggle, and who have laughed at themselves a lot along the way. It's the only part of child-rearing that I'm absolutely certain we got right. I hope our guys were paying attention.

Help Wanted

IT MAY NOT be fashionable to talk about it anymore, but the need for household workers is growing. For the first time, more women are in college—presumably training to join the workforce—than men, and both spouses already work in more than half of all married couples (compared to one-third in 1970). Most of my contemporaries are swamped with civic duties, teaching in community colleges, going to law school, running an office, "doing photography," opening antique shops, or, like me, being done in by a third child who is on a daily search-and-destroy mission. We need help! But subtle changes have taken place that complicate the relationship between employer and domestic employee, especially if the employer is a semi-liberated, "almost"-working mother from East Texas who still washes clothes with Kleenex in the pockets and who has a husband who routinely drops the rubber band off the newspaper onto the floor, two sons with mud-encrusted soccer cleats, a runny-nosed baby, an insatiable cat, and a sandpile.

The problem has its roots in our childhood. I was no Scarlett O'Hara, and the small house on Melton Street in Texarkana hardly merited servants, but almost everyone we knew then employed a black woman to help with the ironing and the children. My mother worked off and on, leaving me in the care of Pinkie Satcher, who rocked me on her ample bosom to the tune of her church choir's Sunday anthem before putting me down for my afternoon nap.

I knew the maids who worked in my friends' houses as well as I knew their mothers. There was Retha down the street, who made us eat our green beans when I ate lunch with my best friend, Frances, and there was Irma at Kay's house, who let us drink Dr Pepper with our breakfast eggs when I spent the night. And there were maids with names that made us giggle—Preshus, Q.T., and Atruss Bee, who had a twin sister named Bee Atruss. We were innocent racists then. These women sometimes took us for bus rides. They would seat us at the front of the bus and then take their own seats on the first row of the "colored section." They starched our party dresses and supervised us at birthday parties in the backyard while our mothers had their coffee and birthday cake inside. If my mother was working at the newspaper office or needed to go somewhere on a day when Pinkie didn't work for us, she sometimes dropped me at the Satcher house on Peach Street in an unpaved neighborhood just west of ours. If there were dangers in that neighborhood then, my parents were probably unaware of it. But when Pinkie wore an open-collar dress, I always noticed the puffy scars across her chest that my older brother told me were made by a razor. That sort of violence and the loving woman who patted me to sleep with "Fly Away to Jesus" seemed so incongruous that in spite of my curiosity I never asked her what happened.

Retha, the maid at Frances' house, was murdered on Christmas Day the year she was supposed to help serve our extended family's Christmas dinner. We had the big dinner anyway, and, as I recall, in the kitchen afterward everybody regarded it as pretty inconsiderate of her to die and leave us with all those dishes to do. The private lives of our maids mattered only insofar as they inconvenienced us.

Little Rock's Central High and Governor Faubus shocked our sensibilities, and I suppose everybody's relationship with their black domestic help was irrevocably altered whether they acknowledged it or not. It was suddenly no longer possible to assume that black women were *supposed* to be maids, and that they *should* want to be a part of our families, even if we had no intention of being part of theirs. My friends and I were thirteen, and we confronted the Pinkies and the Willie Vees in our homes about the race issue. Perhaps out of fear of losing her job or perhaps because she really believed it, Pinkie answered me, "Honey, they is trashy niggers causin' that trouble. I wouldn't never want you to go to school with no colored churrin." One friend, however, said that her family's housekeeper, Savannah, a strong and outspoken woman, once fixed her with an uncharacteristically steely glare and said, "Miss Sally, I don't really care what they does to us in this life 'cause in the next one it's gonna all be different." "I had the uncomfortable feeling," my friend said, "that Savannah would not flinch to see us all roasting in hell in the afterlife."

A summer in school in Chicago, summer jobs in Washington, D.C., petitions, sit-ins, prayer vigils, and ironic first meetings with black students from my hometown on the University of Texas campus in Austin in the early sixties raised my white liberal consciousness and my sense of guilt about a childhood of "separate but equal" water fountains. Although some of us went out to right the wrongs as VISTA volunteers, most of us married, took teaching jobs, and when we had enough money hired our first household workers.

And when we did, we entered a world of conflicting values, where the women's movement was branding housework as "domestic slavery" but where the only way we could escape it to realize our full "potential" was to hire another woman to do it. No matter how much the economists might tell us that service occupations provide millions of badly needed jobs, we still feel, deep down, that our maids are doing work we should be doing ourselves.

We want to think of our domestic help as professionals simply doing a job, but because of the difficulties of race, class, and other perhaps indefinable reasons, both employer and employee seem unable to accept such a matter-of-fact economic relationship. The sixties ended the segregation that made being a domestic the best job a black woman could expect. We can hardly lament that the Pinkies of today are becoming teachers, computer programmers, or lawyers. But the labor-saving devices that helped the post–World War II housewife handle the duties of her household without help aren't much solace to women who now work eight hours a day away from home. And so, even as we need domestics more, we are still trapped between our guilt and the raised consciousness that sends us out into the world. At the same time, the women who traditionally became domestics seem increasingly discontented with their lot.

It is impossible to determine just how many household workers there are in the United States. Because so many domestic employees, and their employers, prefer to sidestep Social Security withholding requirements, their numbers do not show up in any government statistics. According to the 1970 Census figures, however, there are at least 1.2 million household workers in the country, at least 90,000 of them in Texas. Probably there are many more. Of the 1.2 million, 97 percent are black. Texas also has large numbers of Mexican household workers, but because many of them are here illegally or temporarily, it is impossible to know their numbers. In 1970 the median annual income for full-time domestic work was $2,300. Since many of these women are single heads of households, they support their families on this wage.

I've done no specific sociological surveys of household employees in Texas, but my own experience is that employers in Dallas believe there are three general types of domestic workers. (I'll get to what the maids think of their employers shortly.)

The older, experienced domestic worker in Dallas is black, and she comes from East Texas. She may have grown up on a farm around Marshall, Sulphur Springs, or Tyler, and she has probably picked cotton at some time. As hard as it may have been in the country, she has no affection for urban life. She has six or eight children and takes pride that the last three were born in a hospital instead of at home. Her children's high school or college diplomas line her living room wall, along with a commemorative plate of Martin Luther King, likenesses of Robert and John Kennedy, and photos of her children who have fared well and gone to California. She believes in the American work ethic and is a churchgoing woman who leads the Women's Mission Society or sings in the choir. She is considered "family" by her employer, and perhaps she feels genuine affection for the people she serves. More likely, she knows it is good business to have the employer believe such things. She is satisfied that she has raised her children right, even if one or two didn't turn out like she wanted, and that she has given them opportunities she herself did not have. "They worked so hard because they didn't want us to have to be maids," says one young black professional.

The younger black domestic worker may be of a new generation born in the city, or at least she has been in the city long enough to have no ties with country life. She may wear wigs or a natural, disdain uniforms, and speak in the dialect of urban blacks. Like many of her white contemporaries, she may be lacking in self-discipline and in the long-suffering virtues of the previous generation, who learned frugality in the Depression and who are appalled that people are willing to go into debt to buy clothes and furniture. She wants to be paid in cash at the end of the day and refuses Social Security, either because she is receiving welfare payments that prohibit her working or because she lives only from day to day. Because she cannot afford a day care center, she frequently leaves her children at home alone or with a relative. One of her children often has some chronic ailment that requires her to miss work for the long wait at Parkland Hospital or Children's Medical for free medical care. Her own mother may have emphasized the importance of a good education to her, but the school she attended may have left her poorly trained. Still, with blacks moving into jobs throughout the economy, she may consider being a domestic to be menial and beneath her. If she sees no opportunity in such work, chances are she takes as little pride in it as millions of other workers do who find themselves in jobs they consider beneath their capabilities.

The Mexican household worker usually lives in. Instead of a step down, domestic work in the United States is a great leap forward, out of the grinding poverty she most likely knew in Mexico. Even if her employer pays her very low wages, she still manages to send most of the money home, where it may well be supporting her entire family. She is extremely vulnerable to exploitation, since she probably speaks little English and lives in deep fear of being deported. Upon arriving in Dallas and first meeting her new "family," she may be awed by the luxuries and wastefulness of American life. The kitchen garbage disposal is particularly incomprehensible. Her black counterparts, whose jobs she has begun to usurp in recent years, resent her willingness to tackle any task her employer suggests. She comes from a culture that has always had a large domestic labor force and that has few of our egalitarian scruples. She may have great affection for her employer's children. One employer told me that the first Christmas she had Mexican live-in help, she felt confident enough to invite her entire family for Christmas dinner at her house. She started the baking early in December and soon noted with dismay that Delores was scarcely cleaning the house at all. She would load the dishwasher after breakfast, make the beds, then withdraw secretively to her quarters in back of the house. Her employer suspected that Delores had a boyfriend. Occasionally the employer scolded Delores, and she had already decided that this live-in would have to go just as soon as they had survived the holiday ordeal. On Christmas morning, Delores appeared with eyes dancing and presented each of the children with beautiful hand-crocheted stuffed animals.

The social life of the Mexican domestic worker may slowly develop as she meets other Mexican live-ins at the bus stop and at church on her days off. Highland Park village becomes her *zocalo,* as she and a girlfriend parade arm in arm toward the cosmetic counters at the drugstore. Her employer may be baffled by her cultural differences. "Manuela looks like a spidery-eyed vamp when she leaves my house on her day off—you know, huge hairdo, green eye shadow, miniskirt, and five-inch wedges, but Monday morning she appears in my kitchen with her face fresh scrubbed, hair in braids, and white uniform," observed one employer.

Although the family she serves may be eager to obtain her papers, she is fearful of being sent back and wants no contact with immigration offices. As she gradually assimilates into the Mexican American culture and learns more English, she may feel confident enough to quit her first job for a more lucrative one. "I always hate to have Consuela serve a party for fear one of my friends will corner her in the kitchen and offer her more money," a friend confided. Maid-stealing is sundering suburban friendships these days.

Regardless of the domestic worker's background, the role she plays now is vastly different from the one she played twenty years ago. Once at a dinner party I met a woman about my mother's age who had eight children. Thinking of my own tribulations with three, I couldn't resist asking, "How did you do it?" "It wasn't so hard back then, honey," she replied, "'cause we had help. I mean *real* help, that came early and stayed until the kitchen was done and kids in bed." From the stories that women of that generation tell, I know that it was not just the extra hours the help worked; it was an entirely different relationship between the employer and the employee. Many domestic workers, especially in fine homes, became the keepers of standards and traditions. One friend who grew up in that sort of household said that when her mother died the traditional Thanksgiving dinner became her responsibility. "I panicked," she said. "Mother had always made Thanksgiving so special. There were certain glasses and tablecloths we used, and I didn't know which were which. And the dressing was an old family recipe that had never been written down. How could I do it? To my rescue came Rose, who had worked for my family for years. She knew it all. Mother had taught Rose everything about caring for our house. The table for Thanksgiving would be set just as it had been for the past twenty-five years." These are the domestic workers whose recipes still show up in Southern Junior League cookbooks.

I suspect that part of the difference with the "real" help then came from the fact that employers themselves were more domestically capable than the women of my generation are. They knew how to wax floors without electric buffers, they made piecrusts and homemade rolls, and they could sew. I have inherited bedsheets and pillowcases from a grandmother who mended everything so beautifully that I think her darned socks could win prizes at the State Fair. My generation puts polyurethane on its wood floors, bakes only when health food fads dictate, and stuffs holey socks and buttonless shirts into the rag bag. Many of us are unfit to train anyone to care for our homes because we've never learned how ourselves.

Of course, there was frequent exploitation of the domestic worker by that generation. Wages were for the most part unconscionable. One woman recalls that her family's maid in Houston used to come in occasionally and say, "You know, Miz Norris, on the bus this morning I heard Effie May sayin' that Miz Brown payin' her girl eight dollars a day now, and Mamie say she gonna get nine dollars startin' next week. I sure be shamed to say on that bus that I ain't making but six." "Well, Annie," the woman recalls her mother saying, "if that talk on the bus is making you feel so bad, why don't you just catch the earlier bus?"

In spite of the exploitation, tremendous loyalty between employee and employer seemed to develop in those days. Of course, loyalty may come easier when you have no alternatives. The domestic worker kept her mouth shut or said what was in the best interest of keeping her job, and we who loved her as only children can love will never know which of her actions were genuine and which required.

Whether for purely professional reasons or as a true member of the family, the domestic worker of that generation frequently saw herself as guardian of the family image. One woman recalled hearing the maid of her childhood answer the phone one day. It was the cleaner calling to see if the lady of the house had any furs to be stored during the summer. "Oh, Miz Crowley don't have no furs," said Mabel. Then, sensing that she had said something a little disloyal, she added, "But she do have a nice cloth coat." My contemporaries experience great turnover in their domestic employees while our parents' generation and their help grow old together. I know women who have employed the same maid for thirty-five years. "Delia and I don't do much around the house anymore. With the kids grown, there's not that much to do. She and I just share complaints about our arthritis and watch *I Love Lucy* together every afternoon."

Many employers of that generation also paternally tolerated a separate moral code in their maids just so long as it didn't interfere with the work. Perhaps this was easier when the worlds of employer and employee were so very segregated. "Gladys is the finest Christian woman I've ever known. She has seventeen children—five of them born after her divorce from Boyd, but I think they're all his anyway," one employer told me. Another woman my age returned to Marshall to visit her mother. Unable to find a vase that the daughter wanted to borrow, the mother sighed, "Oh, I guess Willie Vee took it." "What do you mean, Mother?" the younger woman asked. "Oh, you know Willie Vee has a stealing problem. Your daddy's gotten her out of jail for shoplifting several times, and she takes things around here all the time. Sometimes I just go over to her house and get them back if I really need them." "But why would you tolerate that, Mama?" "Honey, if you could cook like Willie Vee and make your daddy so happy, I'd let you have anything you wanted." "Mama" accepted it the way contractors write off lumber toted home by carpenters and the way office managers understand the inevitability of missing pens and paper.

But my generation is different. Well, some of us are. I still have friends who seem to have been born to a tradition that suffers no guilt about being waited on. These women admit to having an occasional breakfast in bed. Their domestic workers may have been hired through family connections, the Junior League grapevine, or from the little-known bulletin board at the specialty grocery store that delivers to fine kitchens on Lakeside Drive. These housekeepers and cooks always wear uniforms, speak in pleasant, well-modulated voices ("The Kelly residence. This is the maid speaking"), and have always served well-to-do families without ever having to go through an employment service. Since such household workers are increasingly rare, many women are now hiring Mexican domestic workers. Instead of "This is the maid speaking," the phone is now answered, "Eees no here" or "No house." For some employers, having a Mexican housekeeper is like a return to the good old days. "She's creative in serving our family," said a friend. "She takes my children to the park. She plays games with them outside, and even on her day off, the children prefer to play in her room. If she finds a hole in some clothing or in a tablecloth while she's doing the laundry, she mends it without being asked. Even if she's only preparing lunch for my five-year-old daughter, she sets a nice place mat, a linen napkin, and if there are flowers in the yard she arranges them on the table."

Idyllic as it may sound from the employer's point of view, most of my contemporaries can't handle it. If they do have a Mexican live-in housekeeper, they embarrass her by bringing their friends in to practice Spanish or by taking her to their church discussion group on minority problems. And before long, the lines of authority are blurred and the household worker leaves in confusion to find another job.

Some women—particularly those who have the option of staying at home—decide that employing household help is just not worth the trouble. "Frankly, I get tired of the smell of frying tortillas and the Mexican radio station blaring all day," one woman said. "When I had full-time help, I was never at home with my children. And you wouldn't believe how much money I spent. You have to stay gone the whole day when you have a maid because the kids get all upset when you come in and then leave again, and that inevitably leads to aimless wandering at NorthPark," she confessed. "Your life just isn't your own when you have a maid. If you're sleepy and the baby is taking a nap, you still can't lie down because she's got that vacuum cleaner roaring, or you just feel too guilty lying there while she's ironing." Women who work nine to five are spared such dilemmas; they simply aren't at home long enough to feel uncomfortable about having a servant around the house.

The rest of us fall somewhere in between, hiring someone to help with the housework and child care two days a week and feeling guilty about it. Some women can don their tennis clothes and walk out the minute the maid arrives. While they are charging the net, I am still at home frantically fixing a fresh pot of coffee for my helper and checking to be sure her ashtray is clean. Although she doesn't ask, I feel compelled to explain to her before I leave the house that I'll be working all day—no bridge, no beauty shop, no tennis. And as I drive to the library or head for my little garage-room study, I worry that I didn't make any tuna salad for her lunch. I also worry about my child who comes home at noon from kindergarten, who won't eat his lunch and will tell me later that it was because Elva Lee cut his apple the wrong way and left the tail on his sweet pickle. Elva Lee misses three days without calling, and I have to face the fact that I was never cut out to be an executive when it comes time to fire someone.

This is one area where even the most dependent woman cannot defer to her husband. Dealing with the household worker is woman's work. Even when we are paying decent wages, paying Social Security, and providing paid vacations, we can't seem to get over the idea that this woman is still doing us a favor. Perhaps it's our Puritan heritage that haunts us. Idle hands are surely the devil's workshop when they return at the end of the day with two Neiman's shopping bags. Or maybe the feminists are right. American wives and mothers have been doing unpaid, unsung housekeeping for so long that finally we have come to look upon it as undignified, mean labor, as something that could not possibly be a source of pride and satisfaction.

My first experience as employer was no great success. I rejected the vocabulary of the previous generation. I had learned to say "black" instead of "colored." The woman we hired would not be our "maid." She would be a "household worker" or, in most cases, "our friend" who helps with the house. We would call her "Mrs." because we wanted her to know that we respected her and because, after all, she was at least twenty years our senior. Ruth Lewis, silent, wiry, and small, came from the Domestic Position Wanted column in the newspaper. I tried to call her by her last name, but she kept changing it. She worked for a friend of mine as Ruth Allen, and once when I called her at what I presumed to be her residence, I was told that no one by either name lived there. Ostensibly I had hired her to clean my apartment and tend my new baby one day a week, but she was so unlike the Pinkie of my childhood that I never left the baby with her after I returned early the first day to witness her methodically dusting and saying, "I hear ya, dahlin'" while my firstborn wailed in his bed. (After two more babies I myself have learned to keep dusting and say, "I hear you, darling.") I frequently returned home before noon, cooked a hot lunch, and then worried if it was the sort of food that Ruth liked. She broke her glasses and had terrible headaches, so I gave her extra money to buy new ones. When she was hit by a car and came to work on crutches, I did the vacuuming because she couldn't. When she finally called and said that some teenagers had beaten her up, I was so pained by her pitiful voice that I drove to her house and took her some money and groceries. Vicious dogs threatened to tear me to shreds before I got to the door. Her friend answered my knock and said, "Mrs. Lewis was so "po'ly" that she couldn't see me, but she did appreciate it and she sure hoped "they was cigarettes in that grocery sack." I never saw Ruth-Allen-Lewis again.

Many of my friends were faring no better. Some had inherited family retainers who had once served as their surrogate mothers. "She still corrects my manners and tells me to stand up straight," one young woman moaned. All of these young women admitted that they were serving tea to their housekeepers, apologizing for their own sloppy housekeeping, and promising to do better. Ask Lula to wax floors? Never.

One friend reported that she was so intimidated by her Scripture-quoting household worker that she now retreated to the car in the garage to smoke just to avoid another reference from Ladonia about "defiling the temple of God." It was at least six months before we had the nerve to tell Harriet that her employee was also answering the phone, "Praise the Lord, the Murphys' residence." She did garner the courage to dismiss Ladonia when she knelt and prayed aloud for the revelrous guests at their annual New Year's Eve party.

Still another woman confesses that she was so diffident with her household employee that she couldn't ask her to stop eating the leftover roast, ham, or turkey. Instead, she began taking the meat with her in an ice chest when she ran errands.

Even when the relationship between employee and employer is strained, however, a degree of intimacy is inevitable. The woman who empties your garbage, does your laundry, straightens your medicine chest, and, if she arrives early enough, sees your family interacting at the breakfast table may know more about you than your own mother does. Regardless of their disparate backgrounds, two women in the same house week after week will usually know about each other's aches and pains, gynecological histories, black sheep family members, gossipy neighbors, or straying husbands. Once I even heard about a previous employer's hemorrhoids.

In our effort to be friends as well as employers, we frequently find ourselves being the intervenors between our employees and the complex and occasionally threatening world they face outside our homes. Our aversion to the concept of paternalism flies in our face when Effie May has signed a contract to buy an expensive series of books on black history. We can't stand by and let Vera pay eleven cents a week on a burial policy that will provide her a $100 burial if she lives to be eighty, particularly when we learn that the collection man stopped coming as soon as she got sick. "I try not to mess with her life when it involves her own community, but when I see the white system ripping her off, I can't ignore it," one friend told me. Husbands also get called upon to handle legal matters, Social Security problems, immigration papers, etc.

As "friends" we also concern ourselves with the physical and mental well-being of our domestic workers. A working mother with a full-time housekeeper says, "I've told Ruby that when her children and her sick husband get to be too much for her, she can just stay overnight here and tell them I asked her to work. She has so much to worry about and they demand so much of her at home. I just worry that she has no place to get away from it all. We can take a vacation, but she doesn't have that alternative."

Women who have gone through divorces often say that they couldn't have made it without the support of their maids. Nobody seems more willing to commiserate with you over your man problems than a domestic worker. But it isn't just our "female troubles" or our menfolk that bind us together—it's babies. Myrtle Harris and I had more in common than babies, however. We had both grown up in East Texas in Baptist churches. We shared a regard for the small-town life, and I think she forgave me for becoming an Episcopalian as long as I didn't forget Proverbs 22:6. ("Train up a child in the way he should go, and when he is old, he will not depart from it.") Her conversation was full of people who reaped what they sowed and blessed assurance that the Lord was going to show his wrath to the mothers who failed to chastise their children. Myrtle had eight children. Who needed Dr. Spock with that kind of child-rearing expert around? She counseled my friends and saw me through a second pregnancy. When I complained that the fetus always had the hiccups, she smiled and said, "That baby gonna have lots of hair." I called her hours after Drew's birth. Even in a Catholic hospital nursery full of tiny Ramirezes and Martinezes, no baby had a thicker thatch than Drew Mackintosh. My house may not have been spotless, but I never worried about my children when they were with her. "The only difference 'tween me and you when I'm with them babies," she once told me, "is that you birthed 'em in this world."

Secure as I might feel about leaving my boys with such a loving woman, there are aspects of even that relationship that make me uneasy. I do not like to hear children say, "Just a minute, I'll ask my maid." I call her "my friend," the lady who helps us clean our house, and I praise her capabilities in their presence, but I still worry that my children living in this "safe" white suburb will grow up associating all black and brown people with subservient positions. Stories abound about affluent white children who, on being assigned to a class with a black teacher, innocently report to their mothers, "We don't have a teacher this year—just a maid." Of course, considering the power that most household workers seem to have over me, perhaps my children don't see it as a subservient position at all. A neighbor child across the alley once banged in my back door and demanded that I tie his shoes. "My maid is too busy," he said.

"Manuela is a terrible disciplinarian," one friend confided. "I make the children pick up their own toys and clothes, but if I allowed it, she would wait on them hand and foot. With Mexican help there is always the danger that your children will grow up to be brats."

Although these women can work for us less than a year and become "like family," there are those cultural differences that continue to frustrate and divide us. "Why can't she call and let me know she's not coming?" is the most common lament among women who have grown dependent on household employees. Mexican live-ins frequently disappear at holiday time or during the summer. They may give no warning about their departure or return. Dependability is so basic to our way of thinking that we forget that in their lives they may seldom have been able to count on anything.

Our world is undoubtedly just as peculiar to her. I sometimes stroll my baby along with the maids and their charges in my neighborhood. As we pass a massive remodeling job in progress on a neighbor's house, I am about to admire it when one of the black women speaks up. "That's sure a shame what they done to that house. They doublin' the size, and I hear they addin' three bathrooms, and I bet they don't pay the maid a nickel more when it's done." We buy houses that are too big for one person to care for. We have seldom-used rooms that collect dust and silver services on our buffets that seem to exist only to be polished. Once while I was in Austin, I visited with the woman who cooked for our sorority house during my college years. Mary Lou greeted me warmly and asked, "Where you livin' now?" "I live in Dallas not far from SMU," I replied. "That Highland Park?" "Yes," I said, surprised that Mary Lou was so familiar with Dallas. "Ooowweee, that's a terrible place. I used to live there, too. They eat too many course in that neighborhood—so many dishes to wash you be in the kitchen till ten." I assured her that I lived in the "one course" section.

Other aspects of the suburban woman's life must be equally puzzling. "How come she payin' me to baby-sit her children while she goes to work free for mine at the West Dallas Community Center? If she pay me, I'd go baby-sit my own kids, and she could stay home with hers, and we'd all be better off." "Wonder how come she pay to go to some exercise class? If she push this Hoover some here at home, she wouldn't need no exercise class."

Ironically, the household worker may feel sorry for her employer's children. "That chile still wettin' the bed every night 'cause his mama can't hardly wait to get out of the house in the mornin'. I mean, she got her car keys ready when I walk in the door."

She is naturally resentful when she is treated like a commodity. "My boss lady, she say, 'Next Thursday you go work for my sister 'cause we'll be out of town.' I don't like being passed around. I can get my own jobs. I know the kind of people I like to work for."

The most common lament that I hear from household workers is that employers fail to return at an appointed time. "She don't seem to realize that if I miss that four o'clock bus, I be six-thirty gettin' home." The average bus ride for domestic workers in North Dallas is an hour and a half.

One morning I rode the eight-thirty bus from Main Street in front of Neiman Marcus to Highland Park, and here is what I overheard:

"Oooh, I am glad that Texas-OU football thing is over. She give me two hundred limes to squeeze for punch soon as I walked in, then that child who come home from college with that suitcase full of dirty clothes say it all gotta be handwashed. So I say, 'I ain't gonna squeeze them limes and do no handwashin'—no sireeee.' " (There was a great deal of bravado in recounting what I suspect were apocryphal confrontations with the boss lady.) "You gotta do Thanksgivin' this year?" "No, we had it last year. Her sister gotta do it this year and I sure hope I don't have to serve it." "You know Alice works at one of them fraternity houses. That's a good job 'cause you get all them little holidays off." "Holidays is the hardest-workin' days I got." "An' I tol' her I had an appointment and just had to leave at three o'clock Thursday, but she come waltzin' in at three forty-five, and she could see I was angry, so she gets mad too and says, 'What you got to do that's so all-fired important?' I didn't wan' tell her that I needed to get food stamps. She don't need to know my business, so I said, 'Miz Martin, I don't ask you where you goin' ever time you leave this house. I jus' have an appointment—that's all—and now I can't get there.' " "This is my corner. See them pears in that front yard? She don't do nothin' with 'em. They just rot on the ground."

Though people have been predicting for a long time that household workers are on the way out, I found no evidence of that. The Texas Employment Commission says that the domestic labor force is hard to calculate, but what information it does have indicates that the number of domestic workers has remained static over the past ten years. An interviewer in the Employment Commission office conceded that she sees very few job applicants who are willing to live in and almost no one who wants to cook in private homes. "They can make twenty dollars per day as day workers, and although the cook's job is lucrative, no one wants to work until nine at night."

But with so many women working outside the home, we seem to be entering a high-demand, scarcity market. To get some idea of what the future may hold, I talked with Ms. Annie Ray Harper of the Dallas Committee on Household Employment (DCHE). Ms. Harper, who has been a domestic worker for thirty-one years, is a dignified lady who has no regrets about her years as a domestic employee. "I started when I was eleven years old," she said. "I was a child, but I already had the responsibility of taking care of younger children." She is proud of her years of experience and of her skills as an expert housekeeper. To her, wearing a uniform is a sign of being a professional, and though her job was demanding ("If the pencils needed dusting, I dusted them"), she took great satisfaction in being able to keep a big house running smoothly.

The DCHE, which she directs, is dedicated to improving the quality of domestic work and the conditions of employment. It offers a three-part training course, which is funded partly by the Comprehensive Employment Training Act (CETA). A woman who has completed the first course will have received instruction in health and grooming, household skills and work simplification, nutrition, home safety and first aid, pet and plant care, and kitchen management (all things that I never mastered because I took Latin instead of home ec). Women completing the third level will be qualified for "executive" housekeeping jobs. The DCHE then acts as an employment agency to place certified workers. Ms. Harper believes her certified workers should receive more than minimum wage—$20 a day seems to be the acceptable rate for a nine-to-four job. Ms. Harper is insistent that irresponsibility should not be tolerated in household workers. "It's my own personal feeling that television watching and smoking have no place on the job," she said. "I smoke, but none of my former employers know it because I trained myself never to smoke at work. It's just too hazardous around children and fine possessions."

Ms. Harper's idealism about household working was contagious, and I came away from the meeting determined to be a better employer. Monday morning Elva Lee and I would discuss Social Security again; we would talk about sick leave and holidays and working conditions and performance standards. I would quit feeling guilty about the things that I buy at the grocery store that she can't afford. And if she wanted a Diet 7-Up with her lunch, she would just have to bring it with her.

Monday came and Elva Lee didn't show up. She didn't call, and I spent the day wiping baby William's nose, doing laundry, and trying to figure out how I had offended her on Friday. Ms. Harper told me that tolerating irresponsibility in a household worker only serves to downgrade the profession. But Ms. Harper doesn't know how difficult it is for most women to fire or hire a domestic employee. My generation is so intent on preserving everyone's positive self-image that we find it painful to criticize anyone's performance. I never ask the right questions when I interview domestic workers. I invariably talk too much about the importance of my babies' being loved and cared for when down deep in my heart I also want a house that shines and all of the socks matched and put in the right drawers.

It is becoming apparent that we need the housekeeper more than she needs us. Without a domestic worker, the laundry may get done at my house, but it remains unfolded on the dining room table for days at a time. I don't do housework efficiently because my children know that I am an easy touch for a game of Crazy Eight when I should be cleaning toilets. But right now, I need her most for child care when I am working. For my boys, day care centers, even the cleanest, brightest ones, are a poor second to being at home with their bicycles, their sandpile, and the neighborhood gang.

Wednesday came, and Elva Lee appeared with an excuse about car trouble on a trip to Fort Worth. All is forgiven for a while. She assures me that it won't happen again because she is moving to a new apartment and needs money for furniture. I told her that I wish she'd call when she's not coming. And she says she wishes I'd do something about that baby's runny nose and the sand in those boys' shoes. We are mutually dependent.

It's just like Stella said when Mrs. Dubose came in late one afternoon grumbling about her day of volunteer work as a Pink Lady at Parkland Hospital. "You jus' hush your mouth, Miz Dubose. We all got our crosses to bear. You got the Junior League, and I got you."

Pages from Life

TEN WOMEN IN SEARCH OF A GOOD BOOK, A LIGHT LUNCH, AND A SYMPATHETIC EAR.

THE ALGONQUIN BOOK Club met at my house last month. Seven of its ten members were present. An eighth came after a business appointment. Lunch was cold salmon with dilled mayonnaise served in the dining room on Granny Mackintosh's Coalport china. The book we discussed was *Summons to Memphis,* by Peter Taylor. We resolved two items of business: We agreed to be each other's pallbearers, and I agreed to make them look good in this story.

We are not Helen Hooven Santmyer's ladies of the club. Dallas has its equivalents, the Shakespeare Club and the Pierian Club ("A little learning is a dangerous thing / Drink deep, or taste not the Pierian spring"—Alexander Pope), which are steeped in tradition and formality. Some of our club's more industrious members have belonged to clubs like these as well. But the Algonquin Club has no officers, no minutes, no mottoes, no yearbook, and no themes. We conduct no formal business. Our agreed-upon reading list is sometimes altered from month to month. Even our meeting day is flexible, depending on members' work schedules, school cafeteria duties, and car pools. Aside from a bit of Texas female high-mindedness about the importance of reading, we are an anomaly in Dallas, a community that puts a premium on tight, purposeful organization and accomplishment. Once a month for seventeen years we have arranged our lives to accommodate a three-hour lunch and book discussion that has, as far as I can tell, absolutely nothing to do with advancing us socially or professionally.

Some of us were scarcely acquainted in 1970, when the Algonquin Club began as an escape from postpartum depression, brain atrophy, and the isolation of our children's toddler years. The organizing member flatters us by saying, "I just called up some of my brightest friends."

I can't remember if we were being deliberately ironic or wistful when we agreed to call ourselves the Algonquin Club. Nothing could have been further from our provincial, conservative suburban existence than the irreverent, iconoclastic wits of the Round Table at New York's Hotel Algonquin. Had acerbic Dorothy Parker ("You can lead a whore to culture, but you can't make her think") and the rest of that New York bunch acknowledged life west of the Mississippi, they would surely have dismissed a group like ours with a smirky lampoon.

To our credit, we have never taken ourselves too seriously. We are well aware that our gathering smacks of Highland Park Womanness—leisured ladies lunching. In A. C. Greene's infamous short story "The Highland Park Woman," the main character admits that she belongs to a book review club but that she attends only if the meeting is in an interesting house. In the early days most of us lived in not very interesting duplexes or apartments. Lunch was likely to be tuna salad or a five-can casserole. A period of brown bagging was puritanically instituted when we feared that lunch was assuming too great a role in our gathering. Attendance fell off accordingly. Lunch, better than ever before, was reinstituted.

Our reading lists are revealing and sometimes embarrassing. One member swears that at a low ebb our group actually read a biography of Helena Rubinstein, the cosmetic tycoon—I maintain it was *My Young Years,* the first volume of Arthur Rubinstein's autobiography. We have some standards. One member professes to know of a book club in the neighborhood that gradually degenerated to "Stitch and Bitch." They are now known as "Hair and Nails." It is a cautionary tale. Our discussion of ritual fasting in a Gandhi biography once veered off into a testimonial on the effectiveness of the local Diet Center.

Seriously underlined child-rearing tomes and classics that some of us never got around to reading in college constituted our earliest extant reading lists. In one year we juxtaposed readings of William Faulkner's *Go Down, Moses* and Jean-Paul Sartre's *No Exit* with Joan Beck's *How to Raise a Brighter Child,* Haim Ginott's *Between Parent and Child,* and a text called *Parent Effectiveness Training.* Subsequent lists contained Henry James, Dostoyevsky, Dickens, Jane Austen, Flaubert, Shakespeare, and D. H. Lawrence interspersed with best-seller pop-psych selections such as *Open Marriage* and the *Cinderella Complex.*

Each book is assigned to a reviewer or discussion leader, but everyone in the group is expected to read the book. Slackers were discouraged in a note I found appended to a 1978 reading list: "We have resolved to read these books if at all possible. If not possible, those who haven't read the selection should refrain from entering into the discussion in such a way as to elicit a rehash of the plot." That directive was probably prompted by the meeting at which we discussed Katherine Anne Porter's *Ship of Fools.* Midway through an explanation of the elaborate charts that Jane, the discussion leader, had drawn up to keep Porter's myriad shipboard passengers straight, Susan yawned and asked, "Has anybody here been to see *The Red Shoes*?" That soon became our non sequitur code phrase to silence an unprepared member who would lead us astray.

To remain speechless during book club would be a harsh discipline. Consequently, most of us do our homework. I have observed that women, more than men, are prone to take their reading personally, to test their lives against fiction and biography, almost as if every book is a potential self-help treatise. We seldom read for escape. Book discussions among women move rather quickly to juicy personal parallels and seldom linger too long on abstract stylistic points.

Looking back through years of reading lists, I am struck by the diversity of interests within a group so outwardly homogeneous. Our educational backgrounds run the gamut from Southern Methodist and the University of Texas to Vanderbilt and Stanford. We are statistically abnormal in that eight of the ten of us have been married to the same husband for twenty or so years. We are polite, nonconfrontational Southern women, but consensus on book choices has not always been easily achieved. Though we are all in our forties, we still absurdly protect one member by offering caveats if a suggested book contains violent or steamy sex scenes.

In seventeen years, as in a long marriage, we have grown more realistic about our expectations and our group's attention spans. The classics figure less frequently in our lists. A halfhearted recommendation that we tackle the books on the University of Texas' List of Unrequired Reading was soundly defeated last year. Babies no longer lose their pacifiers under our luncheon tables, and this meeting is no longer our only escape from isolation. Most of us have full-time or part-time jobs. Interest in child-rearing books waned several years ago as we observed the member with the oldest children, who had once counseled and consoled us with such confidence, grow strangely silent. Her children had become teenagers. Most of us have at least one teenager now, and while we retain some optimism and offer each other whatever encouragement we can muster, we can no longer be lured into reading anybody's foolproof formula for effective parent-child relationships. Our one childless member, who now flies in from Houston to our meetings, must be exceedingly relieved.

The reading has been only half the story. Because I live in an all-male household that sometimes seems to offer all of the civility, good manners, and respect for tradition that one expects to find in an athletic dorm, I love these women for the window they give me on a more feminine world. Sometimes I view female gatherings with an almost disloyal objectivity and come away impatient for the forthrightness and candor of my men, but more often I relish the thoughtful ways women care for each other. Some of the women in our club are products of girls' schools. Some have mothers and mothers-in-law living nearby. Most of them have daughters. Through them I have some feel for the enviable intimacy and heartbreaking distances that are all part of mother-daughter relationships. Their lives have so much less solitude than mine. Women sandwiched between their own mothers and daughters in the same community seem to have more social obligations, more shopping, more consoling, and more elaborately planned and supervised entertainment to contend with than I do as a mother of boys.

Without daughters, I seldom think to value beautiful possessions as items to be passed on to another generation. My boys might express passing interest in the pawnshop value of a silver fork, but no sentiment. The degree of my isolation from this female experience became clear to me in our club's reading of Peter Taylor's *Summons to Memphis.* The book deals in part with the attempts of grown daughters to sabotage their aging, widowed father's plans to remarry. Group discussion of the plot resulted in members' vowing to ensure that no jewelry or Waterford goblets would stray as a result of our deaths or our husbands' ill-advised remarriages. I wonder if Peter Taylor had any idea that fiction could inspire such action.

Longevity of association has gradually allowed certain liberties within our group. Once when the book club was meeting in the home of a recently divorced member, the book discussion was shelved altogether. "Have you ever thought about moving that desk by the window over against this wall?" one member innocently asked the hostess. It was as if a charge had been sounded. Suddenly the entire group began rolling up rugs, rearranging pillows, throwing out potted plants, and moving furniture. She was beginning a new life, and her surroundings needed to reflect that. Ours was a spontaneous gesture of genuine and intimate friendship.

No one can pinpoint the year we became more than just a reading club. But each of us can remember a time in our lives when, without our asking, the book club materialized to prop us up or cheer us on. When my second book was published, the group asked to host a book-signing coffee in my honor. These women lead busy lives, which are never more complicated than in the early fall, when my book was appearing. The invitation—mailed to their vast network of friends, who bought an astounding number of books—was dropped through my mail slot a week in advance. Our ten names were tastefully printed in gray on the front of an ecru invitation under our name, "The Algonquin Book Club." Inside, the card said, "honoring one of its own." Accustomed as I was to the somewhat haphazard and undocumented nature of our club, this little invitation with our names all lined up so formally in two neat rows was somehow moving. We had been together longer than anybody had noticed.

We are inextricably bound not necessarily as best friends but as women with a gentle shared history. Our lives are intermingled with the plots and characters of countless books. Together we have known love, mystery, friendships, frustrations, fads, marriages, births, aging parents, financial reverses, inheritance squabbles, sullen teenagers, divorce, and death—in fiction, nonfiction, and biography as well as in our own lives.

Ten good women who read can support much more than a casket.

The Timeless Spell of Ferndale

FERNDALE, an old East Texas fishing club established in 1909, is about two hours and forty years from Dallas. Four or five times a year we turn off Interstate 30 at Sulphur Springs and travel through time down Highway 11 through rolling dairy country punctuated by the small towns of Winnsboro, Newsome, and Leesburg. Holsteins, who probably don't know that they're voguish, pose with cattle egrets on lush green hillsides. Once, two Amish girls on sturdy, ancient bicycles, white caps and long skirts flapping in the breeze, passed us and waved. "Wait'll you see it," my son says to his two friends who have joined him for his sixteenth birthday celebration. "It's like a big old plantation house." The old two-story white frame structure with screened-in porches and jury-rigged additions is nothing of the sort, but as we turn at Shrum's Grocery on the road leading into Ferndale, the sunlight dappling through dense shade from overhanging trees does make the approach seem a little enchanted.

I am not a fisherman, so the lure for me is not the elusive ten-pound bass in the lake. It's the escape, the step back in time, and the apparent immutability. The unstated requirement for membership is that one shall have no desire to change anything. Replacing a rotting boathouse required years of heated negotiation. I am confident that oat-bran muffins or croissants will never defile Ferndale's breakfast offerings of hotcakes, grits, or biscuits and gravy. Deep East Texas meals of fried chicken, catfish, hushpuppies, green-tomato-and-onion relish, and blackberry cobbler are served family style at a long wooden table. The kitchen staff will not count calories or discover cholesterol here until the last one of us who is homesick for this country fare is long gone.

Decorators have been kept at bay as well. Accommodations are spartan—pine-paneled dormitory-like rooms, iron beds with plaid wool blankets, and communal bathrooms down the hall. "Keep voices low after 10 p.m." reads the sign in the upstairs hall. The whole place smells of pine, probably Pine-Sol disinfectant, and my 1940's Texas summers. I take a deep breath each time I go, and I am transported to Little River in Arkansas, a summer place visited so early in my childhood that it has no stories, just vague images of pine cabins and screened-in porches, bare feet, adult laughter, whiskey, cards, and (once) a king snake. I like to think that my sons will have stories to go with this smell. They will remember Camp County dogs named Barney, Daisy, and Jeff who retrieved or stole tennis balls, then retreated to the porches for long naps. They will remember O.P., the black man of indeterminable age who patiently baits hooks and untangles the fishing lines of small children on the dock. Looking like a figure in a David Bates painting, O.P. never changes. In midwinter or in beastly August heat, he wears overalls, a heavy flannel shirt, and the same hat. The boys marvel that he chews Levi Garrett but never seems to spit. He is a man of few words, so they listen up in the boat, trying in vain to keep pace with his instructions as they move across the lake. "Worm for this place," he says in his low, raspy voice, and just as they thread the worm and cast, he shakes his head sadly and says, "Shallow water, need a top water."

When we first joined this club several years ago, I thought it might be a nice place to write, and even now I always pack my small portable typewriter, paper, and several books I intend to read. But there are no desks at Ferndale, only rocking chairs, and the book that held my interest in Dallas can't compete here with tiny hummingbirds hurling their iridescent bodies at feeders outside the dining room windows. At Ferndale I want to be a naturalist, not a writer. I read dog-eared books on wildflowers and birds and take walks on pine needle–covered paths. I try to sketch wild blueberries with fuchsia stems and identify native pine, oak, maple, dogwood, and gum. I step idly over a fallen limb in my path and shiver when it slithers off into the brush.

Occasionally someone at lunch will suggest that we should go into nearby Pittsburg to poke through antique shops or to some dress shop called the Cow House Palace. I decline. My afternoon is full. I've spotted someone's sweet-smelling baby who needs rocking on the porch, and I need to watch for the woodpecker. Supper is at six-thirty. I'll take my coffee outside. The frog chorus and the evening star show begin early.

The Good Old Girls

I KNEW I WASN'T exactly on the cutting edge of the movement when a Houston friend's first question upon hearing that I was going to the National Women's Conference was, "What are you going to wear?" Surely that was not the right question for a feminist gathering. (As it turned out, I was wrong, but not for the reason one might expect.) I was certain that across the country women were just tossing a T-shirt, a pair of jeans, and some sandals into a canvas bag and hopping a plane for Houston while I was eyeing my new wool dirndl skirts and trying to decide if I could make it through airport security with my hair dryer. I opted for a little of both—jeans and black turtlenecks and skirts and neat blouses; I reasoned that at a Mississippi delegation caucus some lipstick and a straight hemline might serve me better than media credentials. However, taking two wardrobes made my luggage so cumbersome that, in spite of the collapsible carrier I had bought to get me independently through the airport, my typewriter proved too much and before I boarded the plane at Love Field I had already enlisted the services of two gentlemen. Settled in my seat, I tried to assume the proper feminist perspective. My male seat companion was a big help: he spent the better part of the flight, with no encouragement from me besides an occasional nod, telling me how indispensable he was to his company and how he was becoming nationally known for his race-car-engine rebuilding. I wondered to myself how long it might take a professional woman to develop such a monumental ego.

I had been instructed by some jaded reporters that to cover a convention it was necessary to write your story before you arrived, then afterward change the things that didn't go as you expected. But I hadn't had enough dealings with the women's movement to do any predicting. The cab ride into Houston gave me time for some theorizing, however. While Texas women, as all women, have had to contend with unequal pay for equal work and inequities of that nature, I was of the opinion that the reason the feminist movement didn't sweep Texas like a storm in its early days was because it concerned itself with certain things that many Texas women had taken care of a long time ago. Maybe it's our frontier heritage; after all, it was the frontier states that first granted women suffrage in this country (Texas was seventh). Maybe our great-grandmothers were just too important to everyone's survival to take much put-down from their men. All I know is that as I grew up in Texas it never once occurred to me to think of myself as inferior to men. Indeed, in Texas high schools the strong tradition of football tended to short-circuit the academic energies of the good old boys while we good old girls who didn't have the legs for baton twirling were busy making the honor roll, editing the school newspaper, and running the student council. Chauvinistically, I wanted to believe that the leaders of the women's movement had set this conference in Texas because we had a tradition of resilience and effectiveness that other women could learn from. Although I knew its goals were more specific, perhaps in a psychological sense this would be the Texanization of the women's movement.

This gathering of women in Houston was bringing together nearly two thousand delegates elected in meetings in every state and territory of the United States. In the next three days, November 18 through 20, the women would forge a twenty-five-point program aimed at eliminating barriers to equality for women. The National Plan of Action, which would include economic issues as well as the controversial issues of the Equal Rights Amendment, abortion, and lesbian rights, will be presented by the conference commissioners to Congress and President Carter by March 21.

Since I was in town a day early, I wanted to get a look at the behind-the-scenes preparations. I saw women acting as security guards, floor tellers, microphone facilitators; they ran first-aid stations and information booths; they acted as interpreters for foreign visitors and non-English-speaking delegates; they signed for the deaf, typed braille for the blind; they provided transportation, housing, and child care, registered the press, and coordinated special events at the Albert Thomas Convention Center and throughout Houston. Most were Texas women and experienced workers coming out of such organizations as the YMCA, League of Women Voters, American Association of University Women, and National Council of Jewish Women.

The press would be looking for radical, braless, denim-clad feminists and, although it would certainly find them, it would also find blue-haired grandmothers, young club women in well-cut suits, and female executives from federal agencies—all being led by Mary Keegan, the chair for the Houston committee of the IWY (International Women's Year) Commission. Mary, who has headed many volunteer efforts in Houston, would be responsible for more than two thousand volunteers, a job few corporate executives would consider taking on at top salary, but which she did without pay.

At the IWY office, the scene was like any campaign headquarters the day before an election—confused. The difference was that women running a national convention like this for the first time are defensive about being called disorganized, so I was quickly taken aside and shown the overall structure for reassurance. With only one day left before the torch from Seneca Falls, New York, would be relayed to Houston, last-minute decisions had to be made, but at this critical point the lines of authority were becoming tangled between the Texas volunteers and the mainly East Coast IWY staff. Only two days before, the national IWY staff from Washington had descended on the Houston headquarters. I sensed that the transfer of power to Bella Abzug, presiding officer of the conference, and her paid staff had not been entirely smooth. While the transition between advance staff and permanent staff is undoubtedly difficult in any large organization, the East / West cultural differences in this exchange of power served to accentuate inherent problems.

The two women who did the most to mediate such differences and circumvent other seemingly insurmountable obstacles were Houstonians Poppy Northcutt and Helen Cassidy. Each time a crisis was resolved, I heard the names of these two extraordinary Texas women. They had been hired in late September by the national IWY staff to act as "special conference consultants." According to Helen, all the national staff had done in

Houston at this point was reserve the meeting halls and hotels for the actual convention dates. No thought had been given to the sort of details that for most national conventions of any size are planned five years in advance.

Helen and Poppy had six weeks to accomplish miracles. Their previous experience with the National Organization for Women conference three years ago in Houston would prove invaluable, as would their friends and contacts throughout the city. Helen, a lawyer, and Poppy, a trajectory analyst and the first woman in Mission Control at NASA and more recently an account executive with Merrill Lynch, had left their jobs to establish Women's Advocate, Inc., in Houston. The two agreed from the start of their involvement with this conference that Helen would deal with the people and Poppy would deal with the things.

Some of the tasks seemed enormous. For example, the Sam Houston Coliseum leased for the conference had no bathroom facilities for the handicapped. Poppy was able to get an additional stall added in each bathroom, but in order to do it, one regular stall had to be narrowed. "Anybody with hips measuring more than thirty-six who got in line for that one was bound to be embarrassed," Helen said. Braille information for blind delegates and participants had to be put up in various places in the hotels and convention center. Sometimes the job had to be done twice. While touring the meeting halls, one commissioner confided to Helen, "I saw this very right-wing-looking young woman pasting some sort of secret code up in our elevators at the Hyatt." A wrestling match had been booked into the coliseum the night before the women's conference was to open. That left only the early-morning hours for setting up the convention floor plus a press room complete with phones, teleprinters, and typewriters.

One of Helen's many people jobs was acclimating the national IWY staff to Texas' modus operandi. "We had the most problems with the New York women. I told them before they got here that in Texas, we say 'please' and 'thank you' and 'yes, ma'am.' They weren't too sure about 'ma'am.' 'Isn't that how people in England address the queen?' they asked. I assured them that any courtesies they might afford the queen would be standard procedure with any women from Texas or the rest of the South. The New York women wanted to pride themselves on being the roughest, toughest, most outspoken women on the earth, but I assured them although we might be quiet-spoken and polite, we could be vicious when crossed. I suggested that they reread *Gone with the Wind* before they came."

Thanks in large part to the efforts of Helen and Poppy, what didn't happen at the conference was as noteworthy as what did. As it turned out, there was no major dissension between the national staff and the Houston volunteers—just an interesting contrast in approach. I saw an example of one type at breakfast Thursday morning in the Hyatt Regency coffee shop. I invited myself to join two very busy members of the national staff who were arguing, even before their orange juice was served, over who was to blame for a proposed demonstration by the militant handicapped from California. "You knew we'd have a demonstration on our hands. I told you to put the paraplegic woman from California on the committee, but you vetoed my recommendation. You should have anticipated this move. The militant handicapped from California could ruin us. I hear we don't even have ramps to the podium if one of them should speak. Who's responsible for this kind of foul-up?" "Foul-up? What about the dog show that got booked in the press room?"

So much talk of "power moves" and "confrontation" so early in the morning almost made me choke on my grits. By contrast, late that afternoon I met Texan Ann Britt, the convention center decorator, who was directing dozens of union laborers without raising her voice. Ann Britt, who grew up in Carthage with a bunch of brothers, is every bit as tough as the women I had met that morning. The difference was in style. Ann Britt was wearing a frilly dress, her hair and makeup were perfect, her nails were polished, and her voice was right out of *The Last Picture Show.*

"Some of these women I'm dealin' with don't have no more sense than a waltzin' pissant. In Texas we grew up knowing that if you really wanna get somethin' done, you first ask politely and you communicate just as clearly as you know how what you want. I'm the only woman convention decorator in this city and a lot of people don't think it's a job for a woman. But I'll tell you, I've never had a bit of trouble with my guys. Getting these Teamsters to work this convention could have been a real mess; I work with the guys who think we all oughta be barefoot and pregnant, but they respect me and do what I tell 'em. Lookin' nice is part of it, I guess. My mama raised me to care what I look like, and rolling up my hair at night doesn't mean I can't demand top wages in this business." All the women behind the scenes were having to deal with conflict, and it seemed to me that the Texas women who had never lost their ability to communicate with the good old boys who install telephones and unload chairs would deserve a lot of the credit for bringing off this conference.

By the time I returned to my hotel Thursday afternoon, new conflict was developing. Delegates from every state and territory and their luggage were beginning to create an impasse in the lobbies of the Sheraton and the Hyatt Regency. If the male desk clerk at the Sheraton had ever contemplated a sex change, surely it was now. The women were bunching up around the desk and polite inquiries about room reservations had degenerated to "What the hell is going on here?" when it became clear that the hotel would be unable to house even those with confirmed reservation slips in their hands. Everyone seemed to have a different explanation for the hotel snafu and rumors swept the lobby. Some said that the Sheraton and the Hyatt simply overbooked for Thursday. Both hotels had offered the IWY reduced rates because they did not anticipate much business the week before Thanksgiving. Others hinted that when a lumbermen's convention at the Hyatt opted to stay another day at full rate, the hotel was reluctant to evict them. Rumors also spread that right-wing groups had called in and canceled entire blocks of rooms reserved weeks in advance by state delegations. After the conference was over, I thought back on the lobbies full of tired women sitting on their luggage singing "Show me the way to go home / I'm tired and I wanna go to bed," and I couldn't help but wonder how much more contentious the conference might have been had the energies of so many women not been initially spent in fighting for space to sleep.

On Thursday I attended my first press conference with Bella Abzug presiding. Again, I realized I had been wrong to assume that "What are you wearing?" was an inappropriate question for the National Women's Conference. Indeed, Bella met the press at that first briefing in a pink suit. Of course, she wore her trademark floppy-brimmed hat, but this one was a complementary shade of pink. Everybody had apparently given appearances considerable thought. Knowing that Liz Carpenter had been worrying about what to wear for her speech at the opening session—the rose Ultrasuede or the new Molly Parnis—some of her Austin friends sent her a telegram that read, "Re: IWY Meeting. Molly Parnis suit. Must change plans. I own same suit. Bought it first. Plan to wear. Know you'll understand. Phyllis Schlafly." "In the early days," said Jane Hickey, a delegate from Austin, "it was a big deal that you *didn't* dress up. I don't know why, except that it was a lot more comfortable—no panty hose, just old tire-tread sandals. But at some point, I guess about three years ago, somebody noticed that nobody listened if they were looking at your dirty feet. I guess the return of dresses indicates a greater degree of political sophistication. We don't want to just be right anymore. We want to win."

In keeping with that sentiment, as Bella introduced various members of the IWY Commission, she said more about their children and grandchildren than about their professional achievements. She emphasized that many of the issues of this conference would go right to the heart of the grassroots American woman, the homemaker—Social Security laws that discriminate against her, inheritance laws that may reduce her to poverty when her husband dies, displacement when she tries to enter the job market when her children are grown. Phyllis Schlafly across town at the Astrodome certainly had no monopoly on so-called pro-family issues. A cynical *Washington Post* reporter leaned over to me during Bella's press conference and whispered, "I wish they'd get off this motherhood stuff. For the first time at a feminist conference, I'm beginning to feel disenfranchised."

Any national convention is a circus, and it seemed to me that this one had more than three rings. I could have spent the entire four days simply looking at the two thousand women on the convention floor. The diversity in their ages, ethnic origins, and dress alone made the conference a reporter's feast: Oriental women with delicate flower-imprinted buttons bearing the slogan "Lotus Blossom Doesn't Live Here Anymore." Midwestern matrons in polyester pantsuits with yellow ERA scarves proclaiming, "Women's Rights Is As American As Apple Pie," California delegates as varied in appearance as their sign indicated—"Imagination Rules the World," Indian women in tribal dress, Nebraska women swinging bras over their heads with a sign saying, "We Never Burned 'Em." Alabama women in their Sunday best demurely needlepointing Christmas ornaments, Guamanian and Hawaiian women in bright muumuus with tropical blossoms in their hair, and of course young women in traditional feminist uniform—jeans and T-shirts.

The diversity in the press gallery was a microcosm of the larger group. For part of the conference I sat beside a delightfully unjaded reporter named Brenda from Springdale, Arkansas. "Oooh, I just can't believe it," she squealed. "Barbara Jordan is my idol and I'm hearing her right now in person." And sometimes I ended up between the more cynical journalists from the East whose entire store of nouns, verbs, and adjectives derived from a certain Anglo-Saxon verb that still retains some shock value in these provinces. At one of the evening sessions, after listening to more than eight hours of floor debates, I wearily remarked to my female press companions that I thought the cause of women's rights might be better advanced if we all turned our voices down about fifty decibels. "I know it's heretical to say, but I've about had it with women today. I don't care what Gloria Steinem says. I am not missing 'the part of myself that society has repressed.' What I'm missing is men, particularly my husband." My companions shrugged coolly, and later when they asked me to save their seats, I asked, "What paper are you with, just in case the press aide tries to seat somebody here?" They grinned, and one offered me her card; it read *Lesbian Times.*

Those "exotic issues," as former Democratic chairman Bob Strauss used to call them, occupied one ring of the circus. My friends back home might feign some interest in the parliamentary maneuvers that brought about the passage of the minority rights resolution, but the main thing they'd want to know was "Did you see any lesbians or prostitutes?" Of course I did. I went to the press conference held by the National Gay Task Force. Jean O'Leary, a commissioner for the IWY, was the spokeswoman for the group and, for the record, she does not have green hair and horns. In fact, that press conference was one of the least sensational I attended. The motto for the lesbian participants was "We Are Everywhere," and out-of-the-closet lesbians proudly displayed their unity by wearing bright orange happy face buttons proclaiming, "It's fun to be gay." From a group that sometimes calls to its defense the homosexual artistic geniuses of the Western world, I found the happy face buttons a real letdown.

The prostitutes showed more imagination. Their group, COYOTE (Call Off Your Old Tired Ethics), described as a "loose women's organization," wore buttons on T-shirts that read, "The trick is in not getting caught." At their press conference I presumed the major issue would be decriminalization of prostitution, but before I knew it I was drawn into a pragmatic exchange on such subjects as zoning of red-light districts, the exploitation of prostitutes by massage parlors, the economic necessity of getting rid of pimps, and the need for massive VD screenings. "It's about time everybody quit blaming the whores for venereal disease," the spokeswoman said. "It's the teenagers who pass that around, and it's bad for our business."

In my attempt to soak up all the diversity of the conference, I missed one of the major events, the last lap of the torch relay that had begun in September in Seneca Falls, the birthplace of the women's rights movement in this country. It must have been impressive; I heard a man say later at the ERA fundraiser that it was the only time in his life that he was sort of sorry he wasn't a woman. Sometimes it was difficult to take seriously a conference that was trying so self-consciously to be historical. Bella and the other presiding officers were banging a gavel once used by Susan B. Anthony, tape recorders were set up in the convention center for delegates and participants to record for posterity their musings on the days' events, and conference memorabilia would be tagged and shipped to the Smithsonian. However, I confess to getting teary-eyed at the opening session in the midst of the drum and bugle corps, the trooping of the colors, the comely young women with the torch, the three first ladies, and the "Battle Hymn of the Republic."

Texas had a strong grip on the opening sessions. Helen Cassidy, again behind the scenes, also had to hire a band for the conference. By that time she was so harassed by the out-of-staters (she now referred to them as "the aliens") that when the bandleader asked about music, she said she told him to play standard convention fare—"You know, 'The Yellow Rose of Texas,' 'The Eyes of Texas,' 'Texas, Our Texas.' " When the Equal Rights Amendment resolution passed, the delegates found themselves singing, "The ERA was passed today [clap clap clap] deep in the heart of Texas." But more than the music, there was the presence of Texas women on the platform—Lady Bird Johnson and daughter Lynda Robb, IWY commissioners Gloria Scott and Liz Carpenter, and keynote speaker Congresswoman Barbara Jordan.

Liz Carpenter's speech to the opening session was full of her characteristic humor, dramatic flare, and remarkable timing. Convention speeches are traditionally ignored, but everybody listens to Liz. "The President of the United States and the Congress have asked us to assess our needs, assert our worth, and set out goals for filling the legislative gaps. I thought they'd never ask!" she opened. She traced the role of women in America from Queen Isabella, who put up the money to discover it (the Native American Indian caucus would take Liz to task for that later), to Sacajawea, who led the pale-faced men to the Pacific. She spoke of women's traditional role as mothers and nurturers but also of the reality of their role as breadwinners; "I have known the warmth of a baby's laughter and, as a journalist, the satisfaction of a newspaper byline." She had strategically stationed delegates of diverse backgrounds on the platform behind her and proceeded to rally the audience like a tent revivalist. The women stood as she related their stories. "Eighty-five-year-old Clara M. Beyer of Washington, D.C., retired government worker of sixty years, protégée of Justice Brandeis, teacher at Bryn Mawr College, one of the handful of valiant women who with Eleanor Roosevelt and Florence Kelley pushed the reform of child labor, mother of three sons and twelve grandchildren. Would you deny this senior citizen mother the Social Security rights due her, or deny women like her inheritance rights?" The crowd roared, "NO!" "The delegate from Minnesota—farm woman Mary Ann Bruesehoff, who runs her own poultry farm on Route Two near Watkins. She was butchering ducks when I called. 'I'm just a chicken picker,' she says. While her husband raises pigs, cattle, and sheep, she just fell into raising three thousand broilers, ducks, and geese each year because, 'We like good old-fashioned food that's uncontaminated.' Everyone else did too and it helps pay the college tuition of three children. Would you keep this woman out of business because she wouldn't get equal credit to run a business?" Again the crowd exclaimed, "NO!"

And then there was keynote speaker Barbara Jordan. You know the voice. One cannot escape feeling a little like Moses receiving divine instruction on Mount Sinai when she intones the Scriptures. "Who can find a virtuous woman, for her price is above rubies . . ." Who could munch popcorn while she demanded, "What will you reap? What will you sow?" Other speeches may have contained noble thoughts, but with a convention crowd it's delivery that counts, and the Texas speakers knew how to deliver.

But the Texas influence extended even beyond the podium. I do not think it was accidental that the Texas delegation was seated on the presiding officer's right at the very front of the convention hall beside microphone number one. Although some might argue with validity that this delegation was not entirely ideologically representative of the state as a whole, few delegations could claim such nearly perfect ethnic or age balance. Delegate Owanah Anderson of Wichita Falls had presided over the Texas state meeting last June with a tomahawk. First names like Lupe, Pokey, Melva, Nikki, Hortense, and Hermine only hint at the diversity of backgrounds confirmed in last names like Glossbrenner, Tobolowsky, Rodriguez, and McKool. The delegation had its well-known faces, such as Nikki Van Hightower, Houston's former women's advocate under Mayor Fred Hofheinz; Eddie Bernice Johnson, regional head of HEW; and Sarah Weddington, now general counsel to the Department of Agriculture, who gave the seconding speech at the convention for the controversial abortion resolution. But within the delegation of fifty-eight Texas women, there were politically astute women that I had never seen before.

I followed Irma Rangel, the first Mexican American woman elected to the Texas Legislature, to a Hispanic caucus one evening between two sessions. Irma has been a teacher in South Texas, South America, and California. Since graduating from Saint Mary's law school in San Antonio in

1969, she has served as a law clerk and assistant district attorney and now maintains a private practice in her hometown of Kingsville. With no education, her father rose from farm worker to barber's apprentice to barbershop owner and finally to landowner and entrepreneur. Her mother also began as a field worker, but by the late forties she was running her own dress shop. Irma is one of three successful daughters. One of her sisters is a pharmacist, the other a teacher. She told me, "Because my mother and father had to work so hard as equal partners to get where they did, I guess my mother was always 'libbed up.' We grew up so accustomed to racial discrimination, I don't think it ever occurred to us to think that we were also being discriminated against as women." Although raised a Catholic, during her stint as assistant DA in Corpus Christi, Irma saw enough suicides and illegal abortions resulting from pregnancies caused by incest and rape to have no qualms about her affirmative stand on the abortion resolution at the conference. Irma's decision to run for the Legislature was prompted in part by the Women in Public Life Conference at the Lyndon B. Johnson School of Public Affairs two years ago. "I saw that there were plenty of black women moving into elected positions, but no Chicanas."

The Hispanic caucus, composed of Cuban, Puerto Rican, and Mexican women, was exasperating to Irma. The room was crowded and noisy. Some of the delegates did not speak English, so the parliamentary process was slowed by the need for occasional translation. "¡Hermanas, por favor!" shouted the presiding delegate in an effort to restore order. Although these women all wear the "Viva la Mujer" button of Hispanic solidarity, I was amazed at the rivalry and difference of opinion within a group that most Anglos would presume to be monolithic. Adopting the blanket term "Hispanic" had consumed the better part of one caucus. "Get to the point, Graziela!" yelled one delegate as a Puerto Rican woman basked in the attention afforded her by chair recognition. "We have one hour to come up with an amendment that meets all of our needs. I want to get goddammit down to work."

Irma worries that many of her *hermanas* know so little about parliamentary procedure. "If they would just read the rules," she says, but then she mellows. "Most of them have so little time to read anything and at least here they can learn by doing." I had seen presidential assistant Midge Costanza at a previous Hispanic caucus. When asked if she thought the Latina representation at the convention was adequate, she candidly replied,

"No, I don't, but what is happening here today—women becoming vocal and organizing—assures that it will never happen again."

I had breakfast with another member of the Texas delegation, Arthur Beatrice Williams of Wichita Falls, who in 1970 was both the first black and the first woman to be a bailiff in Texas. Once a domestic worker, she is currently the secretary to the Wichita County judge. Arthur Bea's main concern at this conference is child care. Having raised a child without a father, she knows the hardships and needs of working mothers. She is a self-assured and able spokeswoman for her causes. "I don't know what it is about me, but I know that people listen to me in Wichita Falls."

When I first talked with Arthur Bea, she was unsure how she would vote on the issues of lesbian rights ("sexual preference") and abortion ("reproductive freedom"). When I talked to her later, she admitted she surprised herself on both of them. "I was tempted to vote against the lesbian resolution, but then I said to myself, 'Arthur Bea Williams, look at your black face. If these women say they've been discriminated against for something they were born with, how can you vote against it?'" On the abortion resolution, she said, "I voted against it. Oh, abortion isn't what bothers me. It's the government paying for it that I don't want. I call it 'sin tax.' I think the decision to have an abortion is a heavy enough burden without asking somebody else to pay for it. But my main concern is that it will siphon money from other medical care. I just have a soft spot for children and old people. I want them cared for first." When I asked Arthur Bea about the value of the conference for her, she said that she'd made some friends and allies. As a member of the mayor's committee on the status of women in Wichita Falls, she hopes with the help of these new contacts to get a rape crisis center established.

The face of a third Texas delegate, Travis County commissioner Ann Richards, may be well known in Austin, but I had not met her before the Houston conference. On Saturday, Ann would second the primary resolution of the conference, the Equal Rights Amendment. In her seconding speech, she said, "I rise in behalf of my two daughters who cannot find women in the history texts of this country. I also rise in behalf of the men, the contemporary men of America in thirty-five states who had the guts to stand up and ratify this Equal Rights Amendment. And I also rise on behalf of the men who are keeping our children tonight so we could be here." She later told me that she called her husband after the speech. "I told him I had done a little takeoff on the Abigail Adams famous entreaty to her husband, 'Remember the ladies.' I said, 'Remember the men.'" "That's nice," her husband replied. "I just watched Phyllis Schlafly do the same thing on television tonight. She thanked her husband for letting her come to Houston."

Ann Richards is said to look a little like Betty Grable or Mitzi Gaynor, but she also has a sort of Texas frontier woman swagger. Actually, she reminds me of Barbara Stanwyck in *The Big Valley* ordering rustlers off the place. When she belted out "guts," every journalist within earshot scrambled for her pen and asked, "Who is that woman?" Ann has been active in politics since her days as a Young Democrat on the University of Texas campus. When she and her husband lived in Dallas, she vented some of her frustration at being kept out of the mainstream of politics ("Alphabetizing cards was about as far as we got in those days") by writing and producing satirical skits with the North Dallas Democratic Women, her first successes as a fund-raiser. When the Richardses moved to Austin, Sarah Weddington called. "She was planning to run for the Legislature but was a political neophyte. It was perfect timing. I needed something, and she needed something I could offer." Ann ran several successful campaigns, for Sarah and other people, before launching what I've been told was a textbook campaign against a longtime incumbent for her present position as county commissioner.

I asked her about women politicians and how they differed from the men she had worked for before. "Well," she said, "women tend to be more receptive to instruction, they don't have to be the boss, they are more interested in new approaches, and they are hesitant to attack." The combination, according to Ann, is a very good package. "Most good women candidates come across as honest, sure of themselves on issues, but also as gentle and as people you can work with." Having observed the Texas delegation in a caucus the night before, I was curious as to where those women gained their political expertise. It seemed to me that a lot of the women in the delegation were club women, business and professional women, members of the American Association of University Women, or perhaps past PTA presidents. She agreed that was true in the beginning, but now Texas women were becoming a political force in their own right. "We looked on our early victories as miracles or accidents, but our subsequent victories have been very calculated, planned, and are not accidents at all. We know now that it takes skill and very hard work."

Ann is the mother of two sons and two daughters. She says that her feminist concerns are in part the result of her position as a daughter and a mother. Her mother belonged to the Rosie the Riveter generation, women who learned during World War II that they could do men's work. "Those women," said Ann, "just like the ones at this conference, did not go back to their homes the same."

But it isn't just what she inherited from her mother, it is also her concern about her own daughters that explains why she's here. Jill Ruckelshaus, the 1976 IWY presiding officer, had said earlier of her generation, "We were raised in the tradition of our grandmothers, but we are living in the tradition of our daughters." Ann agreed. "When my oldest girl brings home a paper from school saying that she can be on the drill team or the pom-pom squad only if her bust does not exceed a certain measurement or if she's not too tall, I am beginning to ask why."

Even before the first plenary sessions, Ann Richards clearly recognized that this conference would be a chance for women to demonstrate their political skill and discipline. She and many of the Texas delegates would work hard with the Pro Plan caucus dedicated to keeping the agenda moving at all costs. Seated so near the microphone, the Texas delegates knew well the power of the parliamentary phrase, "Madam Chair, I move the question."

This National Women's Conference is, of course, unprecedented, but occasionally during the four days I had the feeling that in some small way I'd been there before. The American Legion Auxiliary will probably deplore this comparison, but sixteen years ago I was a delegate to Bluebonnet Girls' State in Austin. Although the Girls' State conference was ostensibly designed to teach us the workings of state government, the majority of us haven't set foot in a caucus room since. At both conferences, the mock and the real, I remember being overwhelmed by the talents and energies of women. Absurdly, bathrooms were an issue at both conferences. Opponents of the ERA have repeatedly suggested that the ratification of the amendment will deny our rights to privacy in public bathrooms. At Bluebonnet Girls' State, because our conference was held at the Texas School for the Blind, we were housed in dormitories that had open shower rooms and no doors on the toilet stalls. Sixteen years ago we never thought to question why our male counterparts at Lone Star Boys' State were housed conveniently close to the Texas Capitol on the University of Texas campus, a campus on which many of them would later build political careers.

At both Bluebonnet Girls' State and the National Women's Conference we trooped the colors, swayed to "God Bless America," talked about the greatness of our country, and listened to government officials, but unlike my mock convention of 1961, this time the listeners were from every possible female walk of life: homemakers and prostitutes, government officials and domestic workers, rural farm women and urban lesbians, experienced club women and women who had never stayed in a hotel or attended a meeting run by parliamentary procedure in their lives. The delegates to my mock convention were from the Valley, the Panhandle, and deep East Texas—a more diverse group than most states could muster—but at the National Women's Conference delegates were of every color and ethnic origin in the United States and its territories. Their concerns ranged from the Eskimo woman's dire dependency on whaling for subsistence to the feminist artist from Manhattan who wanted to know why "art" is what men do while "craft" is the term for the creative efforts of women and natives. And perhaps the big difference between this conference and the one I attended sixteen years ago is that the government officials and influential speakers this time around were all women.

The real nitty-gritty of this National Women's Conference was not the destruction of the American family (although the late-November timing of the conference makes me suspect there were quite a few Thanksgiving turkeys that didn't get thawed) or abortion or lesbian rights—as Phyllis Schlafly told her followers—nor was it just a confused, disorderly women's wrestling match—as perhaps some of the television coverage implied. It was about women and power, and if every item on the agenda had failed, the impact on the women who participated would not be diminished. A black woman from Alabama could not go away untouched by Barbara Jordan's cadence, "We would not allow ourselves to be brainwashed by people who predict chaos and failure for us. Tell them they lie and move on." Nor would a Puerto Rican domestic worker who sat in a Latina caucus with presidential assistant Midge Costanza be quite the same when she picked up her broom on Tuesday. Young women found role models in women past sixty. At the very least we all had a few new names to drop. I met Sally Quinn of the *Washington Post.*

The impact of the conference will be felt in the organizational abilities and compromise skills that women acquired and demonstrated in the caucuses that the television crews never saw. And the power boost for women will come not only from the passage of legislation that may emanate from this convention (Secretary of HEW Joe Califano has already appointed a task force to study the discrimination against women in Social Security). It will also, and perhaps principally, come from the gradual linking up across the country of "good old girls," as Ann Richards called them, the bright and potentially powerful women who know how to raise money and get grants, women who have perhaps heretofore only talked to each other on the telephone but now have spent four days and a few sleepless nights face to face.

Off with the Girls . . . Uh, Women

"YOU'RE ACTING like a Golden Girl," one of my sons said when we returned to our family room in the lodge. We were vacationing with another family in New Mexico. The mother of the other family, whom I see only twice a year, is one of my dearest friends. What my son dubbed a grade-B sitcom was in truth his mother having a great time with an old friend. "Too much talk," he said, "too much laughing."

My sons don't really know the girly me. When it became clear that I was destined to live in a household of males, a male friend observed that women with sons seemed either to retreat to utter manicured, ruffled femininity or to throw in with the guys and become what he called an "astronaut's wife," with a sensible short haircut and running shoes. I didn't want to be the astronaut's wife, but for maximum rapport in a locker room, one does trim and edit a certain amount of female behavior. ("Cutting the crapola," I believe, is the phrase of choice around here.) I am accustomed to after-school conversations that consist of nothing more than grunted monosyllables: "Bull." "Kicked butt." "Swear?" The vicarious experience of growing up male has been enlightening, but rarely uplifting and strangely isolating. "Now, tell it like a girl," I sometimes beg when a report on a school outing has been reduced to the monosyllable "Sucked."

Something catches in my throat when over the fence I hear the little girls next door singing the sweetest made-up songs to their Pretty Ponies. In April I watched them twirl and flit like butterflies in their pastel cotton-voile Easter dresses. Some brief wave of nostalgia and self-pity washes over me when I see a mother and daughter beside the soccer field playing some sort of hand jive rhyming game that I think I used to know. "Down by the river where the green grass grows . . ." I probably couldn't even select a decent hopscotch rock. I miss the company of females.

Women getting away together is a relatively new phenomenon for my generation. Less than a decade ago, an all-female dinner party was downright exotic. Our mothers had to wait until they were widowed. Men have had their poker nights and fishing trips, but women traditionally have headed to the beach or the mountains with the whole family in tow. The change of scenery is nice, but routine housekeeping chores are unavoidable and often must be performed with primitive appliances.

An occasional getaway with women friends is a marvelous respite from that constant surveillance of other people's physical and emotional needs. Women my age with an overdeveloped sense of responsibility rarely take the time to do as they please, but midlife seems to be an important time to indulge ourselves in whatever experiences strengthen female friendships.

Most of my friends figured this out years ago. I revel in their tales of raucous pre-Christmas road trips to Laredo. I have a couple of friends who admit to having graduate degrees in Border shopping. As one who invariably emerges from the *mercado* with two bullwhips, a switchblade, and four masked rubber wrestlers, I marvel at the exquisite bracelets, folk art, linens, and pottery that their well-trained eyes instinctively select. "Too much laughing," my sons would say of the female camaraderie fueled by too many margaritas in the Cadillac Bar after a shop-till-you-drop marathon. They do not want to hear that proper ladies who went without lunch have been known to slide right under the table clutching painted boxes and murmuring, "I'm just sick about the way we're acting."

Some of my best memories are female getaways to foreign climes. Once

I joined eleven women on the all-night train from Laredo to San Miguel de Allende. The train was dirty and the toilet facilities didn't work, but with ample food and limited drink, we rumbled comfortably enough through the moonlit desert and mountains. We still giggle to remember the porter, David (Da-*veed*), in starched white coat, who with some flourish folded down my bed as if we were on the *Orient Express.* He gestured grandly toward the small lavatory, demonstrated the tap, which did not respond, shrugged, bowed, and said with great dignity, "Buenas noches, Señora." One bed fell off the wall during the night, but no one was crushed. On the third day, we wore rubber animal noses to dinner, and the final night all of us performed a spontaneous talent show, to the delight, I'm sure, of the other hotel guests. One of them, a Canadian fellow, said to me at breakfast, "I have never seen women have so much fun. Is it only Texas women who can do this?" Maybe.

Foreign travel with male companions is invariably fraught with a layer of tension that makes real vacation difficult. He worries about getting taken in the money exchange. "I thought your French was better than this," he says. "Actually, I seem to remember your *fluent* Spanish couldn't even prevent the *jefe* in the parking lot in Matamoros from washing our car a second time," she counters. "We've been through this roundabout three times. Shall I drive?" he asks. "Please don't ask the guard if the fishing is good at Giverny. We're here to see the Monets."

None of this petty stuff with women. The week I spent in Paris with my college roommate in August 1985 deserves stars in the Michelin Guide. After accompanying our husbands to the American Bar Convention and traveling the English countryside with five reluctant, ungrateful sons, we felt unleashed *sans famille* in France. She had a good sense of direction, and I spoke enough French to get us in trouble.

We paid homage to the shimmering Impressionist painters, heard Bach, Telemann, and Vivaldi in the perfect acoustics of St. Etienne du Mont, and pillaged the lingerie department at Au Printemps. In the Jardin de Luxembourg, a young Sartre in a black coat too heavy for August tried to sell us his French edition of *Ulysses.*

We sat in the Tuilleries with cappuccino and *tarte Tatin* as often as we pleased. We made up stories about the people passing by and wondered if we had ever been young enough, tall enough, or thin enough to wear a black leotard minidress topped by a wrinkled linen blazer and a hank of wildly tangled long hair like the pouty French ingénue we observed in the mirror of our favorite bistro. Could we yet become the world-weary but still sexy *femme d'un age certain* who dined alone at a table near us under the solicitous and affectionate eye of the handsome maître d'?

Back on the streets of the Left Bank, we squinted to read the tile street signs on the buildings and worried that the next time we saw Paris, it would be through bifocals. Rebelling against that day, we smiled and flirted shamelessly with a table of young Frenchmen at the tiny restaurant Pantagruel in the shadow of the Eiffel Tower. The only sustained attention we attracted was that of a ten-year-old boy, who acknowledged our broad smiles by making monster faces—an appropriate response, as we later discovered in our hotel mirror that the blueberry *coup de glace Vosgienne* dessert had turned our teeth a ghastly shade of blue.

My good friend did not kick my ankle, as my husband surely would have, the night we dined with French friends. With one preprandial champagne, my French was so improved that I attempted to tell *en français* a joke with a punch line that relies totally on an English pun for its humor. By the end of the evening, after a Cognac, she says, I resorted to speaking English with a French accent. I am certain that she is wrong about my singing "The Seine" in the Metro at 2 a.m.

Even physical hardship apparently cannot detract from the pleasures of an all-female romp. I know eight women, a.k.a. the Wilderness Warriors, who have taken these getaways to new heights. They have hiked and camped in Colorado, New Mexico, the High Sierras, Montana, and Wyoming. Their mountaineering and white-water rafting are all the more remarkable because most of them grew up, as I did, when only boys merited the real school gym and one could earn pocket money by forging gym class excuses for your girlfriends. For our generation, cheerleading was the only respectable physical workout; basketball, even half-court, could mess up your hair. Approaching fifty, these Warriors now consider a bicycle trip through New England a little too soft. The year their husbands lovingly insisted that they hire a guide for their yearly trek (they had been lost in the Rockies for twenty-four hours the year before), one indignant member of the group distributed strings of faux pearls at the first campfire, to be worn with their khakis. "If we're going to be treated like debutantes," she explained, "we might as well look like them."

As rough as these trips have been, they are nevertheless distinctly female in their high silliness, intimacy, and sense of purpose. Martha, June, and

Susan become "Queenie," "Moon Rocket," and "Snakes" when they've trenched their tents.

If there is girly giddiness in such outings, there is also a peculiarly female sense of purpose, an aura of self-improvement. These women are not flaunting their physical prowess, although it is a point of pride; nor are they interested in one-upmanship. They are determined to increase their physical and mental endurance, to improve their tolerance, to strengthen their bond of friendship, and to keep a sense of anticipation about life by learning something new. Together once a year, they shed all of their urban sophistication to recapture the goose-bumpy sense of wonder that they knew as little girls.

When some women head for the hills, they also journey back in time. Harvard psychology professor Carol Gilligan has pinpointed age eleven as a time when many women experience what she calls "a moment of resistance, a sharp and particular clarity of vision, an almost perfect confidence in what they know and see." In midlife, it is sometimes restorative to go back to the places where we first experienced that vision and confidence.

For a number of Texas women, the place is summer camp. Each fall, Camp Waldemar in Hunt, Texas, offers a week of retreat and recreation for former campers and their friends. For most of the women who attend, it is a weeklong slumber party full of practical jokes, costumes, and surprisingly serious athletic competition. For others it is a nostalgic reexamining of a place where time once seemed measureless, friendships were instantaneous, and promises were forever and ever. Inspiration untainted by cynicism left us breathless, and life was so full of discovery and abandon that we wrote letters home like this one:

Camp Waldemar
Alameda 4, Summer 1955

Dear Mommy,

We elected leaders last nite. Mimi got senior Aztec leader! I love our counselor Barbara. Our whole kampong is members of the Inca, a tribe we made up. We are crazy.

We were going to play some tricks on G., like sewing up her p.j.'s. We exchanged her drawers with F.C. 1's. When she saw Clare's drawer where hers was supposed to be she said, "I don't give a dam whose clothes these are!" and threw the whole drawer down. She cusses. *We all don't like her.*

Saw a baby snake, found a skull and some bones. Betty got a leech on her toe. It's getting boring so to liven things up I've been riding "Delilah," our dustmop, around.

Did you know that somebody and her boyfriend eloped the other day and got as far as Lancaster and decided to turn back. Isn't that stupid? Some girl here's sister-in-law is expecting in five no four days. She and her husband are 17. That's also stupid!

Yesterday we had more fun in riding. We went on top of Tejas riding hill. It's beautiful there. It was raining all around us. We were laughing and talking and suddenly drip, drip, splash. Boy! We got down that hill fast. When we got on level ground we went faster than I've ever gone at camp. I was riding "Tony" who's real smooth. We ran, actually ran! It was thundering and Barbara was afraid the horses would shy. They didn't but they were very spirited and we could hardly hold them. It rained harder and harder and we went faster and faster. We were laughing and screaming and singing. Mud clods from the horses hoofs hit us but the rain washed it off. We looked like drowned rats. Our hair was plastered down and our shirts were sticking to us. We rode in singing "Why don't it rain on me Mother?" At the kampong we were wild. We had water fights and washed our hair in the rain.

Send me some cream stuff called "Nair" (No hair.)

Love,
Ellen

Being off with the girls can never be quite like that again. My own Mexico traveling companions were reunited at a South Texas ranch. It was no one's birthday, but a piñata swung from the tree. Our good friend who sees to it that we never take ourselves too seriously must have surveyed the gathering of eleven women and surmised that we needed to whack something hard. "Okay," she barked, "line up according to your handicaps. Let's have the most recent divorce up front. Next, anybody with less than two breasts. Somebody with a kid in rehab? Great! How about most recent hysterectomies, then grown kids living at home, followed by parents with pacemakers? Bad real estate investments? Prudence, to the end of the line. You're just worried about your son's SAT scores."

I'm still wondering how much laughter is too much.

Friends

THE PHOTOGRAPH hangs in the hall just outside my bedroom, amid enlarged family snapshots of beach vacations, fishing trips, and birthday celebrations. I wasn't surprised when everyone pictured in it requested an eight-by-ten reprint. Twenty-one adults and eighteen children are seated comfortably on broad deck steps behind the old Austin stone house on an early spring morning in 1982. No face is hidden from the camera. No one's eyes are closed. A baby too young to know she is being photographed cocks her bonneted head toward the camera and smiles anyway. The older children, who range in age from two years to thirteen, display no impatience or irritation at having to sit for this documentation, even though basketballs and sticks in their hands suggest that their play in the backyard has clearly been interrupted. Without exception, the adult faces all express profound pleasure in the moment. There is an almost Edenic air of innocence about this moment captured on an unseasonably warm February day. A small boy in his father's lap holds an apple in his chubby hands. People who notice the photograph on my wall presume it is a family reunion. Well, it seemed like a family at the time.

Now, seven years later, I examine the photograph with a certain wistfulness for the way things were then. The tie that bound me to these people and a handful of others who missed the photo opportunity was ostensibly the workplace. All were related in some way to a young magazine editorial staff. It was a staff that worked and played together for nearly ten years. Since all of them lived in Austin and I lived in Dallas, I could retain my romantic illusions about my friendship with these attractive, witty, talented writers and editors and their relationships with each other. Away from the office politics, the conflicting ambitions and headstrong personalities, I could naively envision our being together forever, offering advice, story ideas, and encouragement, loving on each other's children, gathering on a porch once a year for a photograph while coincidentally producing one of the freshest and sassiest magazines in the country.

It is disheartening to realize that I am still in touch with only five of these people who looked so content together. A sort of diaspora occurred in the ensuing years, sending one to New York, two to California, two to Connecticut, one to Minnesota, and the rest to more-lucrative pursuits or the isolation of novel writing. Some have divorced and probably won't sit together for another photograph, but I stubbornly refuse to acknowledge that they are lost friends. We are temporarily missing connections.

About the time I began lamenting these "missing connections," three old friends, who know that I am the least likely to put any store in palm readers, horoscopes, or graphologists, gave me a visit with a psychic as a birthday joke. All I remember from the hour with this swarthy woman with the hypnotic voice is that I should: (a) surround myself with turquoise (a nice color for any brunette), (b) wear essence of rose perfumes (my husband would leave me), (c) accept "the weeding process," by which she meant losing friends. "You are weeding your garden to prepare for the next level," she explained. "It is painful, but necessary." The hour was up before I could explain to her that I was probably the least ambitious gardener she'd ever met. I want to take everyone, crabgrass and dandelion, with me if I'm going to any other levels.

My tattered address book is a testament to my reluctance to prune.

Here in the *A*'s is the current address of Mary and Peter, the couple that John and I met on our honeymoon twenty-three years ago on a rainy day in Salzburg, Austria. Sharing the same umbrella while we located our cheap *pensione*, we discovered that we also shared the same anniversary, the same silver pattern, and after Pete's job transfer, the same state. They were moving from Pennsylvania to Houston. Our address was Austin at the time, but we welcomed them to Texas as if they were moving in just down the block. We put them in touch with college friends of ours and saw each other two or three times before they were transferred to New Orleans. Mary and I write only at Christmas. I know her three children only from snapshots, but when I passed through New Orleans on a book tour four years ago she brought her good friends into the city to have lunch with me. This is obviously not an intimate friendship. But for some reason, if Christmas came and I did not hear from Mary, I would feel strangely bereft. This once-a-year touching is an important toast to a cozy candlelit meal in a Salzburg rathskeller when we were so young and lonely that we talked openly to strangers, who for an evening at least were our closest friends.

Here in the *B*'s is Jane, who taught with me in an Austin junior high school while our husbands were in graduate school. She was such a fine music teacher that I sometimes spent my free period sitting in class with her students. I never hear Stravinsky's "Petrouchka" or Handel's "Water Music" that I don't think of her. We were scarcely older than our students, but we shared a conviction that if we taught the things we were passionate about, something would stick.

We have seen each other only twice in the intervening years. Her changes of address, coast to coast and back again, have made a mess of my address book. Once during the holidays she and her husband and three children appeared as if by magic, Christmas caroling on my doorstep. Realizing that five years had elapsed since we'd communicated, I telephoned her one February morning. It took several calls to directory assistance in California and Maryland before I located her. She confessed that on her last move from California, she came across a magazine that she had saved because it contained a story of mine. "I really didn't need to be moving old magazines back and forth from coast to coast," she said, but instead of discarding it, she compromised, tore my story out, filed it, and moved it once again. Good friendships, "10's," as Jane calls them, probably can't be "weeded out." Time and distance and space don't seem to make much difference. They may resonate throughout a lifetime. They at least resonate from Texas to Maryland. Jane had spoken my name five minutes before I called.

The rest of the alphabetized address book reveals a host of people who at some point in my life expanded my horizons or who matter to me because I mattered to them. Here is my sixth-grade boyfriend who was my first dance partner, my piano teacher, the organist from my childhood church, someone from my freshman English class, four college roommates, a handful of sorority sisters, two university professors, three coworkers from days as a Washington intern, as well as French and Swedish exchange students who have lived with us. A significant number of names in this address book were my husband's dowry. He says that he had fewer friends than I did because he was not brought up in the Texas public-school-girl tradition of smiling and saying "hi" (with a very flat *i*) to everyone who passes in a school corridor. What he lacked in quantity of friends, I always thought he more than made up for in quality. For me to let go of any of these people would be to let go of a part of the story, a part of myself.

The fact that not everyone feels this way makes me wonder if the trait is peculiar to writers, for whom memory is so important. I talked with a man recently who said that though he lived in the same town with many of his childhood buddies, he never sees them. "I just don't have time to socialize with the intent to get silly. Getting silly was the basis of our friendship. My adult personality doesn't fit back into these friendships," he said with some regret.

Although I have talked to people who admit to having intentionally ended friendships, the whole idea makes me very nervous. But I, too, have lost some friends along the way. Marriages, divorces, children, careers, and just laziness can strain friendships to the breaking point. In at least two cases, I suspect that I've been weeded out. I'm afraid to ask. I would rather believe that my old friends' lives are temporarily saturated with careers and children. Still, when I think how close we once were, I can't help wondering how I misread the relationship. Even worse, I worry that I owe someone an apology for something that I didn't know I did.

That's the problem with friendships. The best ones are a lot like falling in love, but there are never any vows or contracts to establish the boundaries. We may lose a friend by presuming too much, by borrowing too often, or by staying too late, but we may also lose them by being too self-sufficient.

A writer friend of mine once wrote a poignant story of ending a friendship at a shopping mall. Detailing the many ways that she and her friend had gradually grown apart, she concluded that friendship can tolerate almost anything except tact and pity. There is an element of truth in that. I expect a certain amount of candor from my friends, but from time to time, I also expect their forbearance. The older I get, the more I know that none of us gets through life unscathed, and hardly any human relationship can survive without some tact and if not pity, which does connote condescension, then compassion.

Losing friends leaves pangs of regret and guilt, but I don't think it precludes our falling in love again. It's just more difficult in midlife. A tense and exhausting wariness looms over polite dinner parties for middle-aged newcomers. Since I have remained in my home state, my own middle years are cushioned with ancient friendships that were exuberantly and heedlessly embraced twenty-five years ago. Now, as I see us in our forties and jealously guarding our leisure hours, I wince at how cautiously we tease out the potential for a new connection, how tentatively we display our own credentials for possible friendship. "Do we have enough in common?

Should we?" Sometimes the headlong rush occurs, and we come away enchanted with the unexpected fit. But more often we leave social gatherings feeling like the couple in a *New Yorker* cartoon who, as they head for their car, remark, "Well, the Smithsons seemed very nice, but I think we're saturated."

Perspectives on friendships inevitably change with age. My octogenarian father, who claims that he has to serve as a pallbearer once a week, scoffs at the idea of "saturation." "A friend these days," he says, "is anybody who can still walk well enough to get on and off the golf cart."

I'm keeping my tattered address book current and adding some new pages. The "housecleaning" and "weeding" will ultimately be done for us.

Going Home

WE HAVE BEEN traveling for only an hour and a half, but someone is already needing a bathroom stop. We never pass Braum's ice cream shop in Sulphur Springs without stopping anyway. I take them to the rest room, and then wonder if the double scoops they're ordering may end up all over their clothes. We eat our cones in a booth because I don't want the sticky stuff all over my car. I watch their happy faces as they lick their Rocky Road and Butter Crunch Toffee Delight and wet my napkin in my water glass, anticipating the cleanup. I am not traveling with my children. These are my parents. What they once did for me, I now do for them.

I am among the legions of women my age who awaken in the night and groggily wonder if they should be listening for the footfall of a teenager on the squeaky step outside their bedroom that signals a safe return from who knows where or for the tottering to and fro of an unsteady parent who may fall in the bathroom and need assistance. I sometimes forget which house I'm in.

Every four weeks, sometimes more often, I load up on books-on-tape and drive three hours to Texarkana to stay two and a half days trying to refill what is draining out of my parents—life. Just as in twenty years of writing about my own adventures and misadventures as the mother of sons I never pretended to offer my readers foolproof advice, so it is with this time of life. Don't look to me for heroic example. I just stand in the trenches and yell, "This is how it is for me."

On almost any night, you could call me about three a.m. because that's when I get stricken with "The Big Eye." I lie awake and worry about the opposite ends of my family, the ones who are finishing up the race and the ones who are having trouble getting to the starting block. For the past three years, I've intended to finish a book called *No Strings,* about letting go of my sons, which must have seemed imminent when I started writing it. Of course, they're not going. The ultimate letting go is happening at the other end of my family.

My parents have had, and in some ways still have, wonderful lives. For better, for worse, in sickness and in health, after sixty years of marriage, they still have each other. My dad continues to write a Sunday newspaper column to considerable applause at age eighty-eight. My mother, now eighty-five, has been plagued by an assortment of distressing ailments for the past ten years, but well into her eightieth year she maintained a pace that left us all breathless. I, of course, didn't meet her until she was nearly forty. She claims that, at the time, I was not only a mistake; she was sure that I was a tumor.

Her childhood is still a bit mysterious to me. I know that her own mother died when she was three years old, that her house burned, and that she was raised by poor German immigrant grandparents who embarrassed her with their heavy accents. When they died, her father placed her and her sister with an aunt. Her glamorous older sister, Dorothy, ran away from home at eighteen and went to New York to become a showgirl. She toured with W. C. Fields in George White's "Scandals," a popular vaudeville team, married a coal mining heir from Pittsburgh, and eventually died at age thirty-one in Havana. It all seems terribly romantic to me, and I long to know the details of Dorothy's life, but my mother has never talked much about her sister. In fact, the past seems to hold no fascination for my mother. She laughs at my sentimental journeys around old neighborhoods in my hometown. "You must be getting old," she says. "Only old people want to go back to see old haunts."

Only from others did I learn that my mother was the valedictorian of her high school and junior college classes. An old beau of hers who is now an artist living in Mexico told me tales of their salon-like gatherings that included theatrical performances, art shows, and poetry readings.

My father, who grew up as the privileged son of a lawyer, the sort who went off to college in South Carolina in the late 1920's in a yellow convertible, where he spent most of his time and his dad's money booking dance bands and learning the Charleston, claims he first spotted my mother crossing the street in front of the *Texarkana Gazette,* wearing a tight blue knit suit. He was engaged to a Southern belle at the time but was immediately smitten by this smart, sassy young reporter. She became the women's editor at the newspaper and my dad, the night city editor and then the editor in chief. During World War II, she edited the in-house newspaper at the government ammunitions plant, Red River Arsenal. After I was born, she worked off and on when my father needed her at the *Gazette* and the *Daily News*, and I often tagged along. I watched with awe as she moved her thick, soft-lead pencil rapidly through page after page of galley proofs adding commas, deleting redundant phrases, correcting spelling. To keep me entertained while she worked, she taught me how to create a brigade of bayonet-bearing little soldiers marching across a page by typing and backspacing a combination of *o*'s, *k*'s, *i*'s, slash marks, and hyphens. She has never been a June Cleaver or Donna Reed mother. Any cooking skills that I have are purely self-taught. In addition to "soldier typing," I learned from my mother that I was a tolerable speller, a decidedly poor poker player, and a mathematical ignoramus.

Perhaps because she had such a difficult childhood, I think she has always believed that life required great courage. When we were very young and afraid of the dark, she made my brother and me "Brave Hearts," big red construction paper hearts that were pinned to our pajamas to enable us to stare down any boogie men that might be lurking in dark corners of our rooms. A display of squeamishness about a wriggly earthworm or gagging over cleaning up dog doo did not happen twice at our house. Fears and weaknesses were to be confronted head-on and conquered.

If the women's movement did not seem terribly revolutionary to me, it was perhaps because I had grown up in a household and a newspaper office where female intelligence, capability, and even superiority were taken for granted. Others must have shared my opinion of my mother's no-nonsense abilities. She was one of the first women to serve on the formerly all-male grand jury in Bowie County.

Now I wince when doctors or nurses talk baby talk to her. Recently on a jaunt to see an eye specialist in Shreveport, we arrived nearly two hours too early. We opted for a pleasant lunch at Luby's cafeteria and for a stroll in the nearby shopping mall. Because my mother suffered a stroke in 1991, she is unsteady, so I hold on to her as we walk. "I wish you didn't have to hold my hand," she deadpanned as we strolled. "People probably think we're lesbians." Later at the doctor's office, the technician started the familiar litany. "Sweetie, could you lean forward for me? Okay, that's perfect, darlin'.

One more time, princess. Okay, sugar, that's it." "See?" my mother said. "They saw us at the mall. They're all lesbians, too."

My new intermittent role as mother to my mother, as you might guess, is not easily assumed. My father and I readily admit that we're intimidated by this ninety-pound wonder even now. To my suggestions, sometimes relayed in cowardly manner through my father, she responds, "Well, tell her she can go jump in the lake." The stroke took away some of my mother's facial affect, so it's hard to tell when she's amused. The long hospital stays she has endured have taken away a great deal of her dignity. There are a lot of things that she doesn't care about anymore, and that makes me sad. In particular, she does not care about supporting my father's ego. Poor old Daddy complains, "She never laughs at my jokes." In her opinion, my father, my brother, and I have always been a bit too dependent on a good audience.

My older brother, a television anchorman in Baton Rouge, Louisiana, refers to my parents' house in Texarkana as Bosnia. He still gets a laugh out of Mother by saying he's afraid to come visit for fear he'll catch "golden oldie virus." One of the unexpected bonuses in this role reversal is the bonding it brings again with my brother. We now share a closeness we haven't had since he was a rebellious teenager who had to buy his sister's silence. We talk on the phone about once a week, sharing our frustrations with Mother's Great Depression mind-set. Our parents are still saving everything for a rainy day, even though we've had the umbrellas out for years. When I do the grocery shopping, I sometimes lie about the cost of what I've bought and pay for it out of my own pocket rather than own up to the extravagance of fresh asparagus or raspberries, small luxuries I want them to have. My brother and I tip the housekeeper, knowing that she cannot do all that needs to be done in the brief hours that my mother is willing to pay for. When we joined forces to buy my father his first comfortable typewriter chair and decent desk lamp, my mother protested that he wouldn't live long enough to justify the expense. She is persuaded that my father should have stopped buying shoes four years ago. She says, "It's a waste. He doesn't walk much anymore, his foot size is very small, and no one else will be able to get any use from those shoes when he's gone." We fight the battle of the air-conditioning thermostat, and she wins. She even protests my use of hot water in the washing machine and when my back is turned, flips the dial to "cold." I worry that her concern over the cost of medicine will mean that she simply stops taking the expensive pills. But it is instructive for my brother and me to be faced with such frugality. My parents' careful recording of every penny spent flies in the face of our own relative profligacy.

Caring for parents calls forth the old unselfishness you didn't know you could still muster, a Mother Teresa persona that last appeared when a baby kept you up all night and the training pants stopped up the toilet and the older kid begged for one more reading of *Green Eggs and Ham.* With the children, however, there is the gradual reward of seeing them become more independent, less needy. With my parents, I sometimes feel that I am holding their hands on a downhill slide into dependency that I am powerless to stop.

I go to bed at night making lists of just what it is that I'm doing for them. One list reads: cooked some meals, refilled all prescriptions, lined them up in the pill box, mopped the kitchen floor, showed them once again how to play the compact disc player, which my father calls a Victrola, gave my mother a manicure and pedicure, cut my daddy's toenails. While I was on the floor at his feet, he said to my mother, "Look at her, Ruth. I believe she's going to wash my feet with her hair." There is a strong Irish streak in this family—we cannot resist the instinct to see life in a comic light. It is a curse and a blessing—mostly a blessing.

There are other redemptive features to this bounden duty. It forces me to live in the moment, taking small pleasures where I find them. It plunges me into the realm of faith, knowing that I am powerless to make it all right. The burdensome illusion of human control dissolves. The week I expected to have a luncheon for ten, pack a son off to study and work in Mexico, buy a car, and arrange college visits for the youngest son, I found myself instead sleeping intermittently in the Medical Intensive Care Unit waiting room at Wadley hospital in my hometown. "It is good to have all the props pulled out from under us occasionally," says author Madeleine L'Engle. "It gives us some sense of what is rock under our feet and what is sand."

I arrive at the hospital in time to hold my mother's hand as hospital attendants whisk her from Emergency to Intensive Care. Mother has developed heart congestion, and despite all of our rational signing of living wills, by the time I get there, she had already told the doctor to put her on a ventilator if necessary. For perhaps the first time I see fear in my mother's eyes, and I have no red paper Brave Heart to dispel it.

Daddy has developed a horrible rash and is having dizzy spells. The relief

I see in his face when I arrive is both pleasing and daunting. I assure each of them separately that everything is going to be okay, and I don't believe it for a minute.

People who do all of their birthing and dying in one town or city cannot know the experience that I have of "going home." As I settle into the Intensive Care waiting room with the pillow and sheet an attendant has brought, I am reminded that I have reentered a comforting world of people who had a hand in my upbringing—a Baptist church, old schoolteachers, and even a redneck culture, elements of the rock beneath my feet that, in the rush to embrace a wider world, I sometimes thought I had outgrown.

Wadley Regional Medical Center serves not only our town but also the real backwoods of East Texas and Arkansas. The man sitting by the phone we will all share to keep other family members updated is my age and already a *great*-grandfather. I do the math in my head and figure it is possible with a string of marriages at sixteen. In less than four hours I am one with these people. We are nobody apart from our role as "waiters." We wait to visit our critically ill relatives every four hours. Most of their stories are far more dramatic than mine. I am a willing listener. Echoes of theoretical discussions about euthanasia and quality of life ring absurdly hollow here. What can a debate like that mean to men who pour concrete all day or work on an offshore oil rig and who wear T-shirts that say, "If you're not wasted, the day is"?

Seven grown sons in gimme caps gather to await news of their mother, who has had a stroke. Two of the boys, Roy Lee and Mike, and I sleep for three nights on the couches in ICU with our feet extended into straight-backed chairs. They tell me about their mama's hard life. "We was burned out three times. Lost everything. Twice was electrical, but one time somebody cut the screen and shot some Butane in there. You know Mama had the same kind of stroke as that President . . . what's his name, Nixon? 'Cept he died and Mama didn't. She's tough."

When I asked them if they hope their mom pulls through despite the fact that she is paralyzed, one says, "Hell, yes, pardon my French, anything's better'n dying. She ain't blind. She kin still look at her grandkids." I tell them that I think their mother must be pretty wonderful, especially since all seven boys have traveled great distances to be at her side. We talk about fishing the Caddo River even after lights-out. When I wake up in the morning, Roy Lee has gone to get me some coffee. His wife, Renay, who I now know has plenty of problems of her own, has just driven in to take a shift. She says, "Does anybody here know Roy Lee Walker?" "Know him?" I quip. "I've slept with him for three nights."

No one obeys the No Eating sign in the waiting room. An obese teenage girl, inexplicably wearing a T-shirt with a huge cow face on it, yawns and says, "I need some donuts." When I tell her that they have sweet rolls in the hospital cafeteria, she wrinkles her nose and says, "No-o-o-o. I mean I need DONUTS—I'M TALKING SHIPLEY'S OR DUNKIN." White, sugary, and fried stuff is an important palliative in East Texas.

Since I can visit my mother for only fifteen minutes every four hours, I am happy for the distraction of this room of people about whom I have actually begun to care. We pass the time talking about Oprah's weight loss and some talk show they claim to have seen about a woman who had sex on a mattress at Dillard's. When an enormous woman shows up in a bathing suit, I ask if there has been a boating accident on Lake Texarkana. "Naw," says Barbara, who shares my couch. "She come in here wearing that yesterday. You know, it's no sin to be poor. I been poor all my life, but you don't have to be trashy like that." An empty bed in the ICU when I return from a shower and a nap at my parents' house scares me. Maybe Barbara's brother has died while I was gone. I want to know the ends of these stories.

I scribble conversation fragments in my journal at breakfast. One man says, "You know, my memory's gettin' so bad I could hide my own Easter eggs." And when we return from our fifteen-minute visits with our sick ones, one looks so shaken that I ask, "Are you all right?" "Yeah," she grins, "I'm all right, but I'll get over it."

My mother survives this scare. My brother claims that she might have gone gentle into that good night had O.J.'s white Ford Bronco on television not caught her eye and jerked her back into wanting to know what happens next.

She is not as interested in life as she once was. Long illnesses bring depression. Finding ways to amuse her is increasingly difficult. She adores the senior-adult minister who knows her well and bombards her with funny, often irreverent unsigned cards. She loves a lottery ticket. I have observed that many Great Depression veterans faithfully fill out Publishers Clearing House sweepstakes materials and will send off for almost anything advertised as free whether they want it or not.

Saint Paul exhorts us to speak the truth in love. My mother speaks her truth indirectly. She complains about the noise my daddy's typewriter makes as he composes his weekly column. She finds fault with the cook and housekeeper we are so relieved to have found. None of us has ever pretended to understand her completely, but I see in her irascible behavior her fear of loss of control and her anger that all of this is happening to her first even though she is younger and has always been stronger than my dad.

But this "Bosnia" is not without its pleasures. My father retains a remarkable interest in life. He borrows a book I got for Christmas called *Preparing for the Twenty-first Century* and continues to talk politics with me on every visit. The old newspaper editor is passionate about the news and wades through a prodigious number of periodicals daily to get ideas for his weekly column. From him I learn the healing benefits of having work to do.

We also talk about religion. My parents have faithfully attended and supported their church for sixty years. They are, however, what one member of the congregation calls "festive Baptists," who, health permitting, rarely turn down the offer of a restorative afternoon cocktail or eschew a foxtrot to Lawrence Welk reruns. My dad listens to my philosophical questioning of the fundamentalist faith I was reared in with interest. He is, after all, the son of a lawyer and a journalist by profession, experiences that, for good or ill, do not predispose one to childlike faith. But at eighty-eight, he is more immediately concerned than I am about "the world to come." My undermining or tinkering with his notions about the afterlife at this point would be irresponsible and selfish. When he told his young minister that he'd been reading skeptics all week, the minister laughed and said, "J.Q., you better get back to your Bible. Your final exams are coming up."

Both of my parents watch the television quiz show *Jeopardy* every day. My mother is the hands-down champion. I am astounded at her recall of foreign phrases she hasn't studied for sixty years. If I'm feeling mischievous in Dallas, where *Jeopardy* comes on an hour earlier, I call my dad with the answer to the Final Jeopardy question just to confound her.

They both take great pleasure in letters. Sometimes I think we must be the last dinosaur family on earth that continues to use the U.S. postal system to "reach out and touch someone." My brother writes to them almost daily. My dad also corresponds regularly with George, a dear old newspaper colleague in Little Rock, who often writes twice a week. George has recently moved to a retirement home and writes bravely from his new world of regimented chow lines and stewed prunes:

Dear Buffalo [my father's college nickname]:

The women here at Pleasant Hills all look like my mother-in-law when she left this old coil at age 87, white and bluish hair, wrinkles like photos of Mars and a variety of walking aids, starting with three-pronged sticks and graduating to four-pronged walkers and eventually to mini-golf carts. The staff director, however, is a real doll, about 57. Oh, to be sixty again! There appeared today a remarkable double for Gertrude Stein with no boon companion to fill the role of Alice B. Toklas. However, I guess a dame is a dame is a dame or whatever.

Whoopee and hooray! There is going to be a luau tomorrow night. Fresh pineapples flooded in this afternoon as I picked up my mail. There is a promise of a roast pig, but no poi on the bill of fare. I ain't going to a luau if they don't serve poi. The yackey hula, hickey dula set will just have to shimmy without Georgie. Besides, it interferes with my cocktail hour which is fast approaching.

Your friend,
George

Long distance phone calls and E-mail from my contemporaries are never as satisfying.

Some nights after I have tucked my parents in for the night, I walk down the hall and look at photographs of some of their happiest days—a wacky costume party at the country club, visits to the White House when Daddy was on the board of the American Society of Newspaper Editors, photos with politicians and movie stars and old dear friends—most of whom are dead now. I wonder what my children will do with these photos and other memorabilia of their grandparents' heydays. Who will remember all of this? The photos are especially poignant to me because I suddenly realize that I am the age that my parents were when the photographs were taken.

I also think about funerals. My parents have come to regard them as the last social gatherings of their generation. My father also sees them as the last competition. "Outlived you," he silently gloats as he takes his seat under the green tent on the fake grass. Funerals are never without their funny moments. My hometown is very Southern, and funerals frequently involve open caskets and receiving hours where people feel compelled to comment on the mortician's art. "She looks so peaceful, so natural" or

"You'd have thought they'd leave her fake eyelashes off for once." Before the service, while the organist and perhaps a soloist tackle "In the Garden" with considerable tremolo, at least one mourner will straighten the bow on the floral tribute with which she'd like to be credited. The funeral home director, who for me will always be the handsome and witty swimming pool lifeguard who never asked me out, will drive the family limousine. He will be appropriately somber, but if the minister's graveside eulogy goes on too long, he'll wink, roll his eyes, and whisper, "Must have paid him too much in advance." While for my own family I would prefer to avoid the overwrought sentimentality and all the clichéd protocol, we won't. It is important to abide by the rules here.

Like the photos in the hall, the funerals remind me that people live rich, meaningful, and loving lives, that they laugh and dance and cry and play the cards they're dealt with remarkable courage, and then, they are forgotten. Human memories are so short. That is why I write. My own children admit that they do not really remember "Papa," their great-grandfather on their father's side of the family, who endlessly galloped them on his knee and gave himself and his funny little dachshund totally to them in their toddler years. They only remember what they see in the home movies we show at Christmas. And what I've written about him in my books.

Despite my sometimes manic attempts to capture on paper the fleeting world I move in, so much is left out. Did I write about Papa's playing the cornet in the Philippines for President McKinley? Did I leave out the death of his young son or his brief career as a parakeet breeder? How much of my parents' lives do I know?

All of this forces me to think about the unlimited, infinite memory that faith affirms, the memory of the Creator. In this Memory, surely no atom of creation is forgotten. Faith affirms that we are always in some sense being loved and cared for by a God who, unlike me, knew my mother and father long before they turned forty. How comforting to know that Someone knows the whole story and will remember us all, Roy Lee's mama, Barbara's brother, George who missed the luau, and even me, just as we really were.